ISO 9001:2000 in Brief

About the Authors

Ray Tricker (MSc, IEng, FIIE (elec), FInstM, MIQA, MIRSE) as well as being the Principal Consultant and Managing Director of Herne European Consultancy Ltd – an organisation specialising in Quality, Environment and Safety Management Systems – is also an established Butterworth-Heinemann author (see Reference section). He served with the Royal Corps of Signals (for a total of 37 years) during which time he held various managerial posts culminating in being appointed as the Chief Engineer of NATO ACE COMSEC.

Most of Ray's work since joining Herne has centred on the European Railways. He has held a number of posts with the Union International des Chemins de fer (UIC) [e.g. Quality Manager of the European Train Control System (ETCS), European Union (EU) T500 Review Team Leader, European Rail Traffic Management System (ERTMS) Users Group Project Co-ordinator, HEROE Project Co-ordinator, ERRI Quality Consultant] and currently (as well as writing books for Butterworth-Heinemann!) he is busy assisting small businesses from around the world (usually on a no cost basis) produce their own auditable Quality Management System to meet the requirements of ISO 9001:2000. He has also recently been appointed as UKAS Technical Specialist for the assessment of Notified Bodies for the harmonisation of the trans European high-speed railway system.

For this book Bruce Sherring-Lucas (MIQA) joins Ray. Bruce was, for many years, employed by British Rail and held many managerial positions (e.g. West Coast Main Line Special Structures Manager, Project Manager for the Eurostar Track, Platforms and Overhead Catenary realignment and WCML Infrastructure Database population).

As a consultant Bruce worked with Ray at Herne European Consultancy Ltd and was instrumental in writing the ERTMS Environmental Specification for the European Railways, producing a generic Quality Management System for the UK dental technology profession and Railway Safety Specifications (for a German organisation specialising in train control systems). He has also been a member of the ERTMS Users Group Reliability, Availability, Maintainability and Safety (RAMS) Team.

Since returning to the railways, as the Network Rail West Coast Main Line Quality Development Manager, Bruce has been responsible for the successful certification of the West Coast Route Modernisation Project to the exacting standards of ISO 9001:2000. This achievement, completed within a multi-billion pound construction project, is believed to be a first within the railways.

To Lynne and the Boys
(Michael, Andrew and Luke)

ISO 9001:2000 in Brief

Second edition

Ray Tricker

and

Bruce Sherring-Lucas

ELSEVIER
BUTTERWORTH
HEINEMANN

AMSTERDAM • BOSTON • HEIDELBERG • LONDON • NEW YORK • OXFORD
PARIS • SAN DIEGO • SAN FRANCISCO • SINGAPORE • SYDNEY • TOKYO

Elsevier Butterworth-Heinemann
Linacre House, Jordan Hill, Oxford OX2 8DP
30 Corporate Drive, Burlington, MA 01803

First published 2001
Reprinted 2001, 2003
Second edition 2005

British Library Cataloguing in Publication Data
A catalogue record for this book is available from the British Library

Library of Congress Cataloguing in Publication Data
A catalogue record for this book is available from the Library of Congress

ISBN 0 7506 6616 1

For information on all Elsevier Butterworth-Heinemann
publications visit our website at http://books.elsevier.com

Typeset by Charon Tec Pvt. Ltd, Chennai, India
www. charontec.com

Printed and bound in Great Britian by Biddles Ltd, King's Lynn, Norfolk

Contents

Foreword

There has never been a time when the demand for quality has been so high! We long ago stopped settling for 'second best' and now expect and demand consistently reliable products or the efficient dependable delivery of services. Out of this demand has come the necessity for manufacturers and suppliers to have some form of auditable Quality Management System. But how can this be achieved?

The aim of *ISO 9001:2000 in Brief* is to provide the reader not only with an explanation of the background, the requirements and the benefits of the new ISO 9000:2000 family of standards but also, at very little expense, to assist organisations (large or small) to set up an ISO 9001:2000 compliant Quality Management System for themselves.

Explanations are kept as simple as possible so as to appeal to students, newcomers to Quality Assurance or the beleaguered executive with little time to come to terms with the subject.

Preface

The ISO 9000:2000 family is an all-encompassing series of standards that lay down requirements for incorporating the management of quality into the design, manufacture and delivery of products, services and software. The family consists of three standards. These are:

- **ISO 9000:2000 Quality Management Systems – Fundamentals and vocabulary** (superseding ISO 8402:1995 and ISO 9000–1:1994). Describes fundamentals of Quality Management Systems and specifies their terminology.
- **ISO 9001:2000 Quality Management Systems – Requirements** (superseding ISO 9001:1994, ISO 9002:1994 and ISO 9003:1994). Specifies the requirements for Quality Management Systems for use where an organisation's capability to provide products that meet customer and applicable regulatory requirements needs to be demonstrated.
- **ISO 9004:2000 Quality Management Systems – Guidelines for performance improvement** (superseding ISO 9004–1:1994 and ISO 9000–2:1993). Provides guidance on Quality Management Systems, including the processes for continual improvement that will contribute to the satisfaction of an organisation's customers and other interested parties.

To achieve its main objectives, ISO 9001:2000 requires the manufacturer, or supplier, to possess a **fully auditable Quality Management System** consisting of Quality Policies, Quality Processes, Quality Procedures and Work Instructions. It is this Quality Management System that will provide the auditable proof that the requirements of ISO 9001:2000 have been and are still being met.

The main parts of the book are as follows:

- What is Quality?
- What is a Quality Management System?
- The history of Quality Standards
- Who produces Quality Standards?
- What is ISO 9001:2000?
- How Quality helps during a product/service life cycle

- Who controls Quality in an organisation?
- What are the purchasers' responsibilities?
- What are the suppliers' responsibilities?
- What to do once the Quality Management System is established
- How computer technology can be used to improve a QMS.

For convenience (and in order to reduce the number of equivalent or similar terms) the following, unless otherwise stated, are considered inter-changeable terms within this book:

- product – hardware, software, service or processed material;
- organisation – manufacturer and/or supplier.

The first edition of *ISO 9001:2000 in Brief* was written during the transition between the 1994 version of the standard and the all new 2000 edition. Consequently, the book was based substantially on the authors' interpretation of the new standard.

Nearly four years have passed since the introduction of the new standard and theoretical interpretation has been replaced with a sound under-standing and experience in the actual implementation of the requirements. Whilst the requirements of ISO 9001:2000 have not changed, *ISO 9001:2000 in Brief* has been revised to reflect experiences gained over the last four years.

The revisions to the second edition of the book include:

- Reordering the quality management system structure to give process maps precedence over quality procedures
- Assistance on how to develop mission statements and policy statements
- Guidance on the mandatory written procedures required by the stan-dard
- A method of setting Quality Objectives
- Amplification on the various components which comprise a process
- Compatibility with other Management Systems
- A summary of the Eight Principles of Management which are applied within the standard
- A synopsis of the 21 responsibilities that senior management must adopt to ensure the successful implementation of the standard
- An entirely new chapter on what to do once you have installed your quality management system, detailing:
  - The principles of continual improvement
  - How to measure processes
  - Utilising Six-Sigma methodology to improve your processes

- Auditing
- How to progress towards certification
- Another new chapter on the use of computer technology in Quality Management, including the benefits of using company intranets to control quality documentation
- A new Annex giving a comprehensive summary of the ISO 9001:2000 requirements and the intent of each clause
- Updated references and contact lists.

We have also taken the opportunity to remove a large amount of cross reference to the 1994 version of the standard, as this should now be confined to the history books.

Introduction

As a challenge we were once set the task of explaining ISO 9001:2000 in less than 500 words. It was this single action that resulted in the creation of this book. So, by way of an introduction we can think of no better way than reprinting our explanation, which could be titled *'ISO 9001:2000 in Extreme Brevity'*!

The principle of Quality Management

A comprehensive and fundamental rule or belief, for leading and operating an organisation, aimed at continually improving performance over the long term by focusing on customers while addressing the needs of all interested parties.

ISO/TC 176

ISO 9001:2000 is the internationally recognised standard for Quality Management Systems. It provides the benchmark against which companies are measured and if found to be adequate, certified as compliant.

ISO 9001 was first released in 1987 and comprised of 20 elements. It was relatively easy for companies to meet these requirements without actually embracing the intent of the standard. In many cases compliance simply meant a badge on the wall and nothing more. The 2000 version of the standard sought to address this issue and many other deficiencies found in the previous standard.

The current standard is much more business focused, aimed as it is at improving an organisation's management system through the application of eight principles:

1. **Customer focus** – Seeking to satisfy the demands and expectations of the purchaser.
2. **Leadership** – Provision of purpose and direction, such that everyone can achieve the organisation's goals.

3. **Process approach** – The logical sequencing of activities to efficiently achieve a desired result.
4. **System approach** – Managing inter-related processes as a system.
5. **Factual approach** – Decision making based on the analysis of data.
6. **Involvement of people** – The proactive participation of all people in promoting the quality ethos.
7. **Mutually beneficial supplier relationships** – The mutual support of an organisation and its suppliers adds value.
8. **Continual improvement** – Constantly refining processes enables an organisation to become more efficient.

These principles are reflected in the requirements of the 2000 version of ISO 9001, which, in addition to general requirements is structured into four main sections:

1. Management responsibility
2. Resource management
3. Product realisation
4. Measurement, analysis and improvement

The model shown below indicates how each of these sections inter-relates and how continual improvement impacts on all aspects of business management.

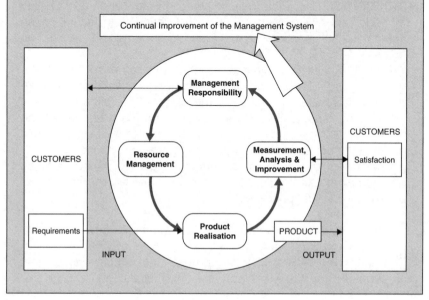

- **Management responsibility**
  The standard requires senior management to *provide evidence of its commitment to the development and implementation of the Quality Management System.*
- **Resource management**
  This part of the standard requires an organisation to *determine and provide the resources needed to implement and maintain the Quality Management System.*
- **Product realisation**
  Probably the most important part of the standard in which an organisation is mandated to *plan and develop the processes needed for product realisation.*
- **Measurement, analysis and improvement**
  No Management System can be effective without a suitable means of measuring its performance. The standard calls for an organisation to *plan and implement the monitoring, measuring, analysis and improvement processes needed* to prove the effectiveness of the Management System and its deliverables.

This short paper provides a very brief overview of the standard and, if that is all you bought the book for, it has served its purpose. However, the rest of this book is well worth a read as it expands upon and explains each of these principles in greater depth.

1 WHAT IS QUALITY?

Why is the word 'Quality' (although an everyday word), often misused, misquoted and misunderstood? Probably this is because when most people talk about the quality of an object, or service, they are normally talking about its excellence, perfection or its value. In reality, of course, they should be talking about how much it meets its designed purpose and satisfies the original requirements.

Take for example a £50,000 Mercedes and a £15,000 Ford. It would be very unfair to suggest that the Mercedes is a better quality car simply because it costs more! Being realistic, both cars meet their predetermined quality requirements because they have been built to exacting standards and are, therefore, equally acceptable as 'quality' vehicles. It is simply that the design purpose and original quality requirements (i.e. the level of quality) differ.

So what exactly is **meant** by the word quality? There are many definitions but the most commonly accepted definition of quality is '*The degree to which a set of inherent characteristics fulfils requirements*' (ISO 9000:2000).

In other words, quality is based upon customer satisfaction. So in the case of the Mercedes and the Ford, a purchaser of a Mercedes will be satisfied only if they get leather seats and cruise control, whereas the Ford driver is happy with crushed velour and a CD player. Their required level of quality differs but each is equally satisfied with their purchase. The characteristics of each car satisfy the customer's requirements.

Consumers, however, are not just interested in the level of quality 'intended' by the designer, manufacturer or supplier, they are far more interested in the delivery of a product (i.e. hardware, software, service or processed material) which is **consistently** of the same quality. They also want an assurance that the product that they are buying truly meets the quality standard that was initially offered and/or recommended.

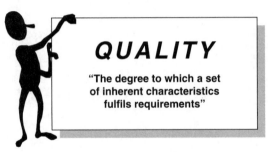

Figure 1.1 Definition of quality

Products of a consistent quality mean that repeat purchases are more likely; something which any car driver appreciates when considering whether to stay with a preferred make and model.

This consumer requirement has meant that manufacturers and suppliers (especially the larger organisations) have now had to pay far more attention to the quality of their product than was previously necessary. Organisations have had to set up proper Quality Management Systems in order to control and monitor all stages of the production process and they have had to provide proof to the potential customer that their product has the guaranteed – and in some cases certified – quality required by the customer. In other words, the manufacturer or supplier has had to work within a Quality Management System (see Figure 1.2 for details) to produce their product or deliver their service.

Unfortunately, with the current trend towards micro-miniaturisation and the use of advanced materials and technology, most modern day products have become extremely complex assemblies compared to those that were available just a few years ago. This has meant that many more people are now involved in the manufacture and/or supply of a relatively simple object and this has increased the likelihood of a production or design fault occurring.

Similarly, the responsibility for the quality of a product has also been spread over an increasing amount of people, which has meant that the manufacturer's and/or supplier's guarantee of quality has, unfortunately, become less precise.

The growing demand for an assurance of quality before a contract is awarded has reinforced the already accepted adage that quality products play an important role in securing new markets as well as retaining those markets that already exist. Without doubt, in these days of competitive world markets, quality assurance has never been more relevant. No longer can suppliers rely on their reputation alone!

Thus the drive towards quality-led production now means that today's purchasers are not just expecting a quality product but are also demanding proof that an organisation is constantly capable of producing quality products or providing quality services. The provision of this proof is normally

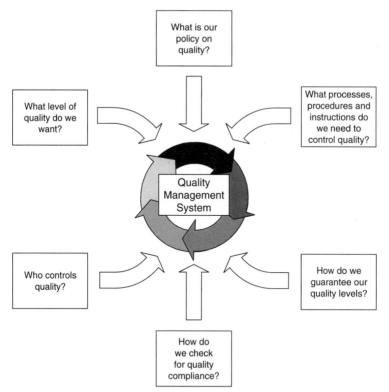

Figure 1.2 Some of the questions answered by a Quality Management System

in the form of an independent third party certification and this is possibly the single most important requirement for a manufacturer, organisation or supplier.

Up until a few years ago, however, there were no viable third party certification schemes available. But with an increased demand for quality assurance during all stages of the manufacturing processes, came the requirement for manufacturers to work to recognised standards, and this is why ISO 9000 was first introduced.

So in summary, 'Quality' **is**:

- giving complete satisfaction to the customer;
- a standard which can be accepted by both the supplier **and** the customer;
- complying consistently to an agreed level of specification;
- providing an acceptable product at an acceptable cost;
- providing a product which is 'fit for the purpose';
- the totality of features or characteristics of a product that bear on its ability to satisfy a given need.

Quality **is not** about:

- complying with a specification (as it is possible that the specification may be wrong);
- being the best (since achieving this ideal may be very costly and could exceed the price that the customer is prepared to pay);
- only producing a product that is 'fit for the purpose' (as that purpose may be completely different to the customer's actual needs).

Quality is all about customer satisfaction!

2 WHAT IS A QUALITY MANAGEMENT SYSTEM?

'A management system to direct and control an organisation with regard to quality.' (ISO 9000:2000)

Let's get one thing straight from the start; a company controls its business through the application of a *business* management system, not as the standard suggests through a *quality* management system. So don't get hung up on the word quality.

Consider if you will, ISO 9001:2000 sets the standard for a business management system which, if implemented correctly, will lead to products and services of a predetermined quality. These products and services will, in turn, satisfy the customer's requirements and expectations.

A better title for ISO 9001:2000 would possibly be 'A Standard for Business Management Systems'. Indeed, a number of companies that have implemented ISO 9001:2000 have deliberately avoided using the term 'quality', preferring instead to simply call their business activities a 'management system'.

ISO 9001........ A Standard for Business Management Systems

Having said that, for the purposes of this book, we will stick with the term Quality Management System, as it is ill advised to upset the International Standards Organisation!

A Quality Management System is the organisational structure of responsibilities, activities, resources and events that together provide procedures and methods of implementation to ensure the capability of an organisation to meet quality requirements.

A successful Quality Management System (QMS) relies on a variety of interactions and inputs within an organisation as indicated in Figure 2.1.

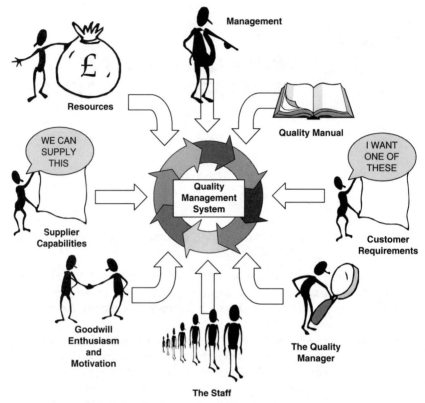

Figure 2.1 The ingredients of a Quality Management System

An organisation having a carefully structured QMS can achieve their ultimate goals for Quality Assurance (QA) and Quality Control (QC).

The first thing that ISO 9001:2000 requires is for an organisation to set up and fully document their position with regard to quality assurance. These documents comprise the QMS and describe the organisation's capability for supplying products that will comply with laid down quality standards. The Quality Manual contains a general description of the organisation's quality policy and provides specific details about the quality assurance and quality control within that organisation.

In order to be successful an organisation must be able to prove that they are capable of producing the product to the customer's complete satisfaction so that it conforms exactly to the customer's specific requirements and that it is always of the desired quality. An organisation's QMS is, therefore, the organisational structure of responsibilities, procedures, processes and resources for carrying out quality management. As such it must be planned and developed so that it is capable of maintaining a consistent level of quality control.

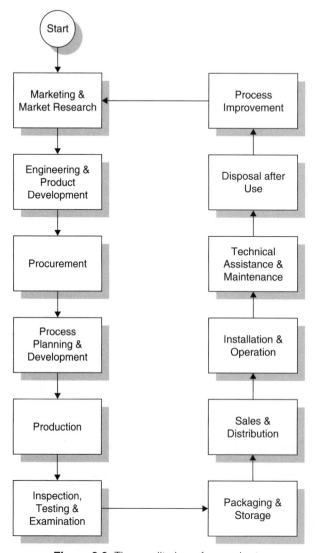

Figure 2.2 The quality loop for products

The 'quality loops' in Figures 2.2 and 2.3 should always be followed by an organisation to ensure that all aspects of the production and supply cycle have been considered in the QMS.

So whether you produce 'nuts and bolts', design software or provide a service (such as public relations), a QMS is ideal for running your organisation.

However, to be effective, the QMS must be structured to the organisation's own particular type of business and should consider all functions such as customer liaison, design, purchasing, subcontracting, manufacturing,

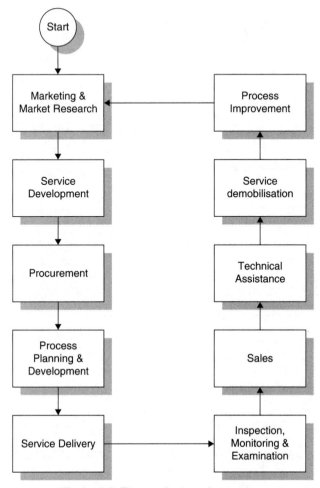

Figure 2.3 The quality loop for services

training, installation, updating of quality control techniques and the accu-
mulation of quality records. In most organisations this sort of information
will normally be found in their Quality Manual.

The type of QMS chosen will, of course, vary between one organisation
and another, depending upon its size and capability. There are no set rules
as to exactly how these documents should be written. Nevertheless, they
should – as a minimum requirement – be capable of showing the potential
customer exactly how the organisation is equipped to achieve and maintain the highest level of quality throughout the various stages of design,
production, installation and servicing.

As an example, some of the determinants and measures of the quality of
a product and service are shown in Figures 2.4 and 2.5.

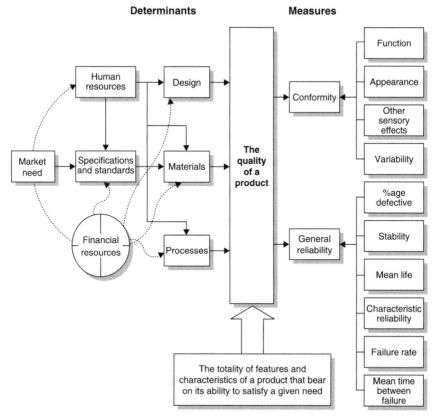

Figure 2.4 Some of the determinants and measures of the quality of a product

2.1 What are the requirements of a Quality Management System?

To be successful, an organisation (whether large or small) **must**:

- be able to offer products that satisfy a customer's expectations;
- deliver products that comply with the relevant standards and specifications of a contract;
- market products at competitive prices;
- be able to supply products or services at a cost that will still bring a profit to that organisation.

Organisations must, above all, provide a quality product that will promote further procurement and recommendations.

So how can your organisation become a quality organisation? Well, it is **not** just a case of simply claiming that you are a reliable organisation and

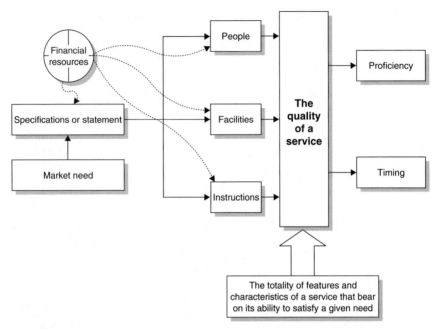

Figure 2.5 Some of the determinants and measures of the quality of a service. (Figures 2.4 and 2.5 are extracted from BS 4778:1979 which has been reproduced with the kind permission of BSI. Although the 1979 edition has been superseded, these figures are included here since they illustrate the concept)

then telling everyone that you will be able to supply a reliable product! Nowadays, especially in the European and American markets, purchasers are demanding proof of these claims. Proof that **you** are the organisation that **they** should be dealing with.

Figure 2.6 No proof of quality ... no business!

How can anyone supply this proof? Well, the easiest, most recognised and usually accepted way is to work in conformance with the requirements of ISO 9001:2000. This standard provides guidelines for organisations wishing to establish their own QMS and thereby control the quality of their organisation – from within their organisation.

Figure 2.7 The benefits of proof

But it doesn't just stop there! Sometimes a contract will require an organisation to comply with the specifications of other standards. (For example, a British component manufacturer might be required to meet BS 3934:1965 'Specification for dimensions of semiconductor devices and integrated electronic circuits', or for a dental laboratory it could be European Community Council Directive 93/42/EEC concerning Medical Devices.) A well-structured QMS can prove extremely useful for dealing with these situations.

As we said earlier, an organisation must **prove** their 'organisation's capability' by showing that they can operate a QMS. Figure 2.8 shows how a QMS benefits an organisation by providing both that organisation and their potential customers with the necessary proof.

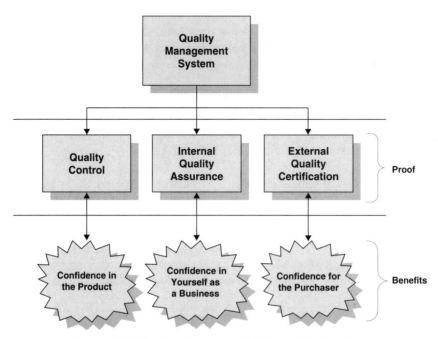

Figure 2.8 Quality Management System – the benefits

To satisfy these requirements, an organisation's QMS has to encompass all the different levels of quality control and quality assurance that are required during the various stages of design, manufacture and acceptance of a product and be capable of guaranteeing quality.

These requirements generally cover the following topics:

- organisational structure;
- measurement of quality assurance;
- contract-specification;
- design control;
- purchasing and procurement;
- production control;
- product testing;
- handling, storage, packaging and delivery;
- after sales service.

2.2 What are Quality Control and Quality Assurance?

Quality – 'The degree to which a set of inherent characteristics fulfils requirements' (ISO 9000:2000).

But what of Quality Control and Quality Assurance?

Although the terms 'Quality Assurance' and 'Quality Control' are both aimed at ensuring the quality of the end product, they are in fact two completely separate processes.

2.2.1 Quality Control

Quality Control (QC) – 'part of quality management focused on fulfilling quality requirements' (ISO 9000:2000).

It is the amount of supervision that a product is subjected to, so as to be sure that the workmanship associated with that product meets the quality level required by the design. In other words, it is the control exercised by the organisation to certify that all aspects of their activities during the design, production, installation and in-service stages are to the desired standards.

QC is exercised at all levels and as all personnel are responsible for the particular task they are doing, they are all quality controllers to some degree or other.

One practical example of QC would be using a calibrated thermometer to ensure paint was cured at a predetermined temperature within a drying oven. The desired standard would be the temperature specified for curing

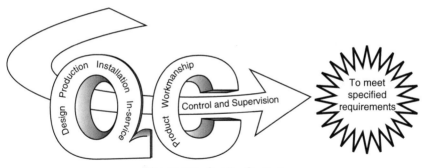

Figure 2.9 Quality Control

the paint, with the thermometer giving the assurance that the standard was being met.

2.2.2 Quality Assurance

Quality Assurance (QA) – 'part of quality management focused on providing confidence that quality requirements will be fulfilled' (ISO 9000:2000).

'Quality'   is fitness for intended use.

'Assurance'   is a declaration given to inspire confidence in an organisation's capability.

'Quality   in a product, by consistently achieving stated objectives, is, Assurance'   therefore, a declaration given to inspire confidence that a particular organisation is capable of consistently satisfying need as well as being a managerial process designed to increase confidence.

QA is also a declaration given to inspire confidence that a product has achieved the intended standards and that its manufacture, installation

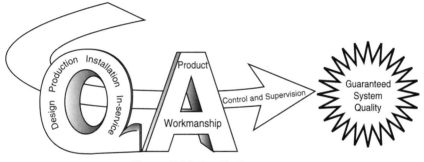

Figure 2.10 Quality Assurance

modification and/or repair has been completed in an efficient and timely manner.

The purpose of QA is:

- to provide assurance to a customer that the standard of workmanship within a contractor's premises is of the desired level and that all products leaving that particular firm are at, or above, a certain fixed minimum level of specification;
- to ensure that manufacturing and/or service standards are uniform between an organisation's departments or offices and that they remain constant despite changes in personnel.

In a nutshell, QA is concerned with:

- an agreed level of quality;
- a commitment within an organisation to the fundamental principle of consistently supplying the right quality product;
- a commitment from a customer to the fundamental principle of only accepting the right quality product;
- a commitment within all levels of (contractor and/or customer) to the basic principles of QA and QC.

2.3 What are the costs and benefits of having a Quality Management System?

'An effective Quality Management System should be designed to satisfy the purchaser's conditions, requirements and expectations whilst serving to protect the needs of interested parties'
(ISO 9004:2000).

In practice, some QA programmes can be very expensive to install and operate, particularly if inadequate quality control methods were used previously. If the purchaser requires consistent quality then he must pay for it, regardless of the specification or order which the organisation has accepted. However, against this expenditure must always be offset the savings in scrapped material, rework and general problems arising from lack of quality. How much an organisation benefits from its QMS is directly related to the money it invests. However, it is always possible to put too much money into quality controls. The optimum benefit comes when the investment in quality controls is balanced against the most significant reduction in the cost of poor quality. As can be seen from Figure 2.11, any further investment beyond this point will not result in substantial gains.

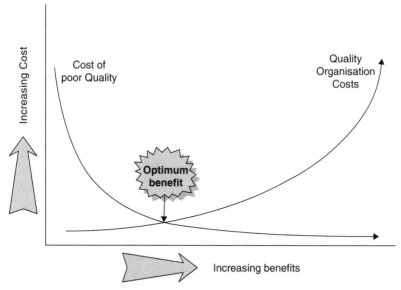

Increasing Cost

Cost of
poor Quality

Quality
Organisation
Costs

Optimum
benefit

Increasing benefits

Figure 2.11 Quality Management System costs

The main benefits of quality management are:

- an increased capability to provide a product which consistently conforms to an agreed specification;

Consistent products to
an agreed specification

Figure 2.12 An increased capability

- a reduction in administration, manufacturing and production costs because of less wastage and fewer rejects;

Production costs

Figure 2.13 Reduced costs

- a greater involvement and motivation within an organisation's workforce;

Figure 2.14 Motivated staff are happy staff!

- improved customer relationships through fewer complaints, thus increasing sales potential.

It was great doing business with you

Figure 2.15 Customer satisfaction

For an organisation to derive any real benefit from a QMS, everyone in the organisation must:

- fully appreciate that QA is absolutely essential to their future;

Quality = More orders = Long term security

- know how they can assist in achieving quality;

Why not ... ?

Figure 2.16 How can your staff assist?

- be stimulated and encouraged to do so.

You're a winner with Quality!

Figure 2.17 Be encouraged by the organisation

With an effective QMS in place, the organisation will achieve increased profitability and market share and the purchaser can expect reduced costs, improved product fitness for role, increased satisfaction and, above all, growth in confidence. But … without an effective QMS, organisations will definitely suffer.

In the following sections we will look at each element that makes up a Quality Management System and how they combine to clearly define how a business achieves its goals.

2.4 What is a Quality Manual?

'a document specifying the quality management system of an organisation' (ISO 9000:2000)

A Quality Manual is a document setting out the general quality policies, procedures and practices of an organisation. Or, put another way, it is an organisation's written record of what they say and do to produce a quality product or deliver a quality service.

An organisation's Quality Manual is the formal record of its QMS. It is:

- a rule book by which their organisation performs its business;
- a source of information from which customers may derive confidence;
- a means of defining the responsibilities and inter-related activities of every member of the organisation;
- a medium for defining the level of quality that an organisation wishes to consistently deliver;
- a vehicle for auditing, reviewing and evaluating the organisation's QMS.

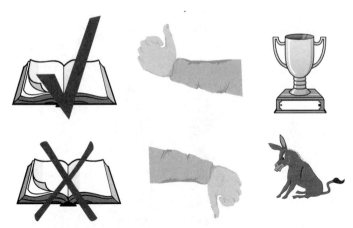

Figure 2.18 A Quality Manual is vital for success

A Quality Manual is the single point of reference required to run all aspects of an organisation to consistent quality levels. It is the heart of a QMS and is essential for anyone considering applying for ISO 9001:2000 certification.

2.4.1 What goes into a Quality Manual?

To be effective, the Quality Manual must:

- include a statement of the organisation's policy towards quality;
- contain details of the organisation's quality management structure and organisation, together with roles and responsibilities;
- describe the organisation's quality control requirements, training programmes, etc.

The Quality Manual will also identify sub-sets of Process Maps, Quality Procedures (QPs) and Work Instructions (WIs) and provide templates of the various forms and documents used by the organisation – such as production control forms, inspection sheets and documents used to purchase components from subcontractors.

QPs and WIs will include details of the specifications which must be complied with. For a manufacturer these may include:

- particulars of drawings;
- supporting documentation;
- tools and gauges that are going to be used;
- sampling methods;

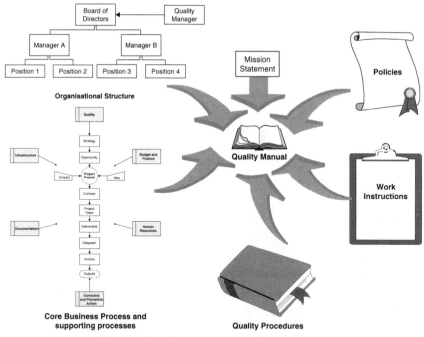

Figure 2.19 What goes into a Quality Manual

- any tests which have to be made;
- test specifications and procedures;
- the acceptance/rejection criteria, etc.

For organisations providing a service the following may be found in their Quality Manual:

- response time criteria;
- service standards;
- customer satisfaction and complaints procedures;
- courtesy requirements (e.g. acceptable telephone manner).

For a complete description and guidance on how to develop a Quality Manual, the reader is referred to ISO 10013 – Guidelines for developing Quality Manuals.

2.4.2 What does each part of the Quality Manual do?

Each part of a Quality Manual has a specific role to play, as shown in Figure 2.20.

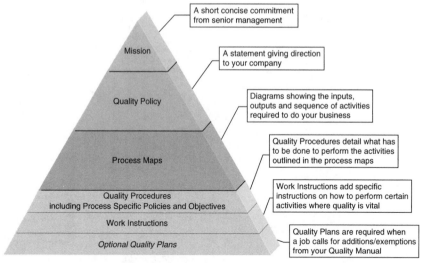

A short concise commitment from senior management

A statement giving direction to your company

Diagrams showing the inputs, outputs and sequence of activities required to do your business

Quality Procedures detail what has to be done to perform the activities outlined in the process maps

Work Instructions add specific instructions on how to perform certain activities where quality is vital

Quality Plans are required when a job calls for additions/exemptions from your Quality Manual

Mission

Quality Policy

Process Maps

Quality Procedures including Process Specific Policies and Objectives

Work Instructions

Optional Quality Plans

Figure 2.20 What each part of a Quality Manual does

The structure of a Quality Manual is expanded upon in the following sections.

2.5 What are Quality Policies and Objectives?

Quality Policy – 'the overall intentions and direction of an organisation related to quality as formally expressed by top management' (ISO 9000:2000)

A Quality Policy is a statement of the organisation's overall quality intentions and direction regarding quality (as formally expressed by top management). It outlines **how** management intends achieving quality and dictates how every other aspect of an organisation's QMS is set up and run.

There are three types of policy statements that an organisation should consider:

- **Mission statement** – A very brief high level statement of intent from senior management;
- **Corporate policy statement** – An expansion upon the mission statement;
- **Process-specific policies** – Clear statement of intent for each process performed by a business.

2.5.1 Mission statements

Whilst ISO 9001:2000 does not call directly for a mission statement, they are ideal as a means of starting a Quality Management System, as they aim to polarise the mind and point everyone within a business in one particular direction.

Mission statements should ideally be instantly recalled. Examples are given below.

We the XYZ Company aim to:

Deliver a safe and reliable oil exploration service that robustly meets the requirements of our customers …

… in a way that:

Discipline, workmanship, & value for money are at the heart of our thinking, planning & doing …

… so that:

The XYZ Company is the 'benchmark' for delivering oil exploration services throughout the industry.

ABC plc will strive to become the leading provider of elastic widgets.

We will achieve this vision through building a business that:

- Applies state of the art processes
- Uses cutting edge materials and equipment
- Has the capability to respond quickly to customer requirements
- Maintains an internal drive for improved performance
- Grows through building upon core competencies

Figure 2.21 A commitment from senior management

All these mission statements have certain things in common, in that they:

1. define a goal for the business;
2. state corporate values;
3. start to define measurable objectives;
4. imply a need for employee competence;
5. address customer satisfaction;
6. point towards continual improvement.

These points should be addressed when writing your own mission statement.

2.5.2 Corporate Policy Statement

If an organisation is serious about setting up a QMS, then senior management must commit themselves by stating their policies on quality. Without a firm commitment from top management, an organisation's QMS will fail. This is usually achieved by the management putting together a policy statement outlining their intentions, based upon their mission statement.

This high level policy statement should be focused on customer satisfaction and:

- be appropriate for the needs of the organisation and its customers;
- involve everybody within the organisation;
- outline the organisation's goals and objectives;
- be communicated and implemented throughout the organisation;
- be understood by everyone.

ISO 9001:2000 unintentionally gives us some guidance in putting together a policy statement; in so much as the standard is based upon Eight Quality Management Principles (see Section 5.5). By establishing your policy against these principles you should end up with a robust statement. Such a policy statement may look like the boxed text shown on the facing page.

ISO 9001:2000 makes no reference to any financial policies, which we feel is an oversight, bearing in mind that all companies strive to maximise profits and minimise overheads. So you may want to consider adding a ninth statement to the effect that you will visibly demonstrate cost effectiveness.

2.5.3 Process-specific policies

The number of process-specific policies you need all depends upon what activities your organisation needs to control. It may be that all you want to do is instil some discipline into your mailroom because the clerks are sinking under a mountain of paper! At the other end of the scale your organisation

The policy of this company is to achieve and maintain a high standard of management in all aspects of our operation and to continually satisfy the expectations of our customers.

We will conduct our business through the following principles:

Customer focus
We will deliver products that comply with our predetermined requirements which recognise the needs and expectations of our customers.

Leadership
We will provide direction for the business by establishing clear objectives that serve to fulfil business goals.

Involvement of people
We will develop our business through the involvement of our staff, by utilising their knowledge and experience.

Process-based management system
We will run our business through a structured process-based management system and will ensure that all our staff works to the requirements of this system.

Management of inter-related processes
We will identify, understand and manage the inter-relationship of our business processes to ensure our operations are effective and efficient.

Factually based decision making
We will make informed business decisions by the analysis of data attained from suitable metrics.

Continual improvement
We will commit to enhancing our management system through the proactive identification and implementation of improvement opportunities.

Mutually beneficial supplier relationships
We will develop relationships with our suppliers and work with them to improve subcontractor performance.

Signed
Managing Director

may be looking to control all aspects of its work. It is your decision, but whatever the reason you must have policies to start getting things under control. For the purposes of ISO 9001:2000 you will be expected to have all your key processes controlled. This standard requires an organisation to break down

Figure 2.22 No policies … no Quality Control!

its activities into a series of inter-related processes that describe how an organisation manages its quality. Once the Core Business Process and its supporting processes have been identified, it is then relatively straightforward to define policies for each of the processes.

The benefits of having a policy for each process are immense, as policy can be clearly dictated against the main activities of the organisation, thereby avoiding any ambiguity.

As a minimum and to comply with the requirements of ISO 9001:2000, you must have written procedures and hence policies to cover the sections detailed below.

The standard is very specific on the minimum number of procedures that must be documented, although there are many more that may need documenting to satisfactorily run your management system.

However, to be compliant with the standard you must ensure you have written procedures on the following:

Section	Title	Intent
4	**Quality Management System**	
4.2.3	Control of documents	Using the wrong version of a design or work instruction can be very costly to a business. Consequently, a process must be developed that ensures you only use the correct version of a document.

Section	Title	Intent
		Furthermore, these documents must be: • approved prior to use; • catalogued to record the current issue in use; • periodically reviewed to ensure they are still suitable.
4.2.4	Control of records	Records are the tangible proof that your management system is being operated correctly. Records must be kept for a specified period of time, in good condition and readily retrievable. Your procedure will detail: • what records are required; • where they are stored and in what medium; • how they can be retrieved; • their retention period and method of subsequent disposal.
8	**Measurement, Analysis & Improvement**	
8.2.2	Internal audit	Internal auditing is a mandatory requirement within ISO 9001:2000 and is intended to prove whether you are doing what you state within your management manual. The written procedure shall identify responsibilities and ensure that non-conformities are actioned without undue delay. You will also require an audit programme to support the procedure, which will specify the frequency and extent of audits.
8.3	Control of non-conforming product	Defective or damaged products must not be used or delivered to a customer. Your written procedure must ensure that these non-conforming products are dealt with in one of three ways: • Defect rectification. Once a defect is removed, the product must be rechecked against the original specification; • Use under concession. A sub-standard product can be used subject to it being formally authorised (usually with the customer's consent).

(*continued*)

Section	Title	Intent
		• Prevention of use. This is usually achieved through quarantine and subsequent controlled disposal (or destruction).
8.5.2	Corrective action	Nothing works perfectly all the time, so when things do go wrong you will need to establish why and find ways to prevent re-occurrence. Once corrective action has been implemented you will also need to review the action to see if it has been effective. Your written procedure will, therefore, include the identification, investigation, rectification and verification of corrective action.
8.5.3	Preventive action	Preventive action involves predicting the causes of potential failures (non-conformities) before they occur. Clearly preventing a non-conformance is cheaper than rectification after the event. There are numerous methods that can be applied but risk assessment is more desirable than a crystal ball! As with corrective actions you must record the results of actions taken and review the effect of preventative action.

Whilst these are the only *written* procedures the standard demands, you are at liberty to set down in words as many procedures as you feel appropriate. Remember, procedures are generally used to amplify the detail shown on process maps. You may, therefore, choose to process map the mandatory procedures in addition to those maps you have prepared for carrying out your core and supporting business activities. Conversely, you can add detail to the core and supporting processes by writing procedures.

A closer inspection of the standard would suggest that there are, through implication, two other procedures that should be documented, these are:

• **Customer Communications** (7.2.3)
  (which states *'The organisation shall determine and implement effective arrangements for communication with customers'*)
• **Purchasing process** (7.4.1)
  (which states *'Criteria for selection, evaluation and re-evaluation shall be established'*)

Just a word of warning; no one likes to read procedures on how to do things. Process mapping is the better option as it visually represents your

Figure 2.23 A picture paints a thousand words!

business. Keep written procedures to a minimum and only use them when they are either mandatory (see above) or will add value and clarity to a process map.

2.5.4 How to set Quality Objectives

Quality Objective – 'something sought, or aimed for, related to quality.' (ISO 9000:2000)

As ISO 9001:2000 tells us, quality objectives are established to provide a focus to direct your business. The intention being to lay down the desired results you wish to achieve and how to apply resources to achieve these goals.

Quality objectives need to be consistent with the high level corporate quality policy and in turn relate to the process-specific policies.

There is one basic rule that needs to be applied when setting quality objectives, that being, think 'S.M.A.R.T.'

- **S**pecific
- **M**easurable
- **A**ttainable
- **R**ealistic
- **T**imely

Objectives must be concise and to the point. Wishy-washy statements such as 'we will be the best' are unrealistic as there is no way of telling whether you are the best in the business.

A statement such as 'We aim, by the end of this fiscal year, to deliver 99.8% of all our products within 48 hours of receipt of order' meets the

S.M.A.R.T. criteria as follows:

- **Specific** – The objective relates to a physical activity, in this case the delivery of a product. Consider a specific objective as one that can be observed and therefore verified against predetermined criteria. In the above example 'product delivery' is the observable action and 'within 48 hours' is the specific criteria.
- **Measurable** – The objective is capable of being measured, as targets have been set through percentages and timescales. A mechanism can therefore be put in place to capture this data, be it a dispatch note that records departure and arrival time of the delivery van or, in this high-tech world, a satellite tracking system which automatically records when the van arrives at its destination. In essence you need a dependable system that can measure your success in achieving the objective.
- **Attainable** – Clearly this company is confident that it can deliver 99.8% of its products on time; therefore the objective is in their opinion attainable. Ideally such an objective should be agreed by the staff that are performing the activity, since if you have only provided them with a delivery bike with a flat tyre, they may not agree that 99.8% is attainable! In any instance the target must be sufficiently demanding to ensure the delivery team are not wasting time and therefore becoming inefficient.
- **Realistic** – This must not be confused with Attainable. Realism in this context means whether the objective is realistically applicable to the people responsible for performing the task. In the example above you would not ask the delivery team to increase profits by 5% over the next fiscal year. However, by asking them to deliver 99.8% of products within 48 hours of receipt of the order should lead to customer satisfaction and therefore repeat orders, which in turn should improve the financial bottom line. In short apply specific objectives to those who are capable of delivering them.
- **Timely** – No great surprise here. There is no point in setting an objective without specifying a time by which it should be achieved. Our delivery company has given themselves until the end of the fiscal year to attain their objective.

Objectives that are S.M.A.R.T. can be monitored. In this way you will be able to establish whether you have been successful in achieving your goals, or conversely, if you have failed to meet them, you will be able to quantify the failure rate, identify ways in which to improve and ultimately set new objectives.

2.5.4.1 How to go about setting measurable objectives

Simply ask yourself what influences the way in which a procedure is performed. These 'influences' are the known variables that will either make the procedure succeed or fail.

For example, beer manufacture is influenced by the type of hops, the yeast, temperature, brewing time, shelf life, etc. All these influences can be considered as success criteria. So if your objective is to make consistently acceptable barrels of beer, then it is not difficult to see that it is important to measure the criteria that impacts upon your success as a brewer.

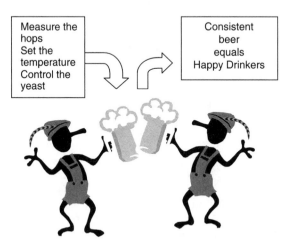

Figure 2.24 Measuring success criteria leads to meeting objectives

2.5.4.2 Fancy a RUMBA?

For those of you with a love for acronyms you may like to consider the alternative to S.M.A.R.T., that being R.U.M.B.A. Whichever way you choose to generate your objectives, the same principles apply.

Reasonable	You are capable of meeting the requirement within current rules, regulations and legislation, i.e., it will not put you behind bars!
Understandable	You understand what the objective is aimed at achieving.
Measurable	The objective can in some way be monitored to see that it is meeting its intended target.
Believable	Your staff feel that it is a realistic objective and will therefore strive to meet it.
Achievable	The objective is theoretically possible.

2.6 What is a Quality Process?

Quality Process – 'a set of inter-related or interfacing activities which transform inputs into outputs' (ISO 9000:2000)

Figure 2.25 What is a process?

Processes can be found all around us. Take for example the process of getting up in the morning. The initial starting point (input) would be you sleeping in bed. The alarm clock would carry out the process of waking you up, which would be followed by the action of getting up (the output). The alarm clock (the process) would then need to have some quality controls (such as checking that the clock is telling the correct time before going to bed, setting the wake up time and ensuring the alarm is switched on) to ensure that the process will work.

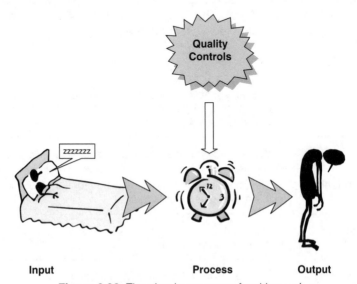

Figure 2.26 The simple process of waking up!

An example of a more complex process would be building a computer network, where inputs are both human and physical. The method of combining the skills of the technician, the component parts of the system and, most important, meeting the customer's requirements, are controlled by a process specifically developed to deliver an acceptable result (i.e. the output).

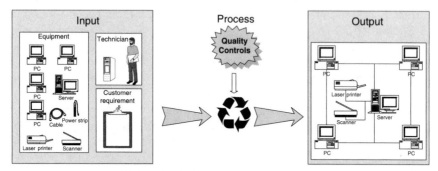

Figure 2.27 A more complex process

2.6.1 The Process Approach

Any activity that receives inputs and converts them to outputs can be considered as a process. Often, the output from one process will directly form the input into the next process.

For organisations to function effectively, they will have to identify and manage numerous interlinked processes. This systematic identification and management of the processes employed within an organisation (and particularly the interactions between such processes) is referred to as the 'process approach'.

In addition to inputs, outputs and quality controls, processes comprise of suppliers, customers and the resources needed to perform the process. A more accurate depiction of a process is shown below.

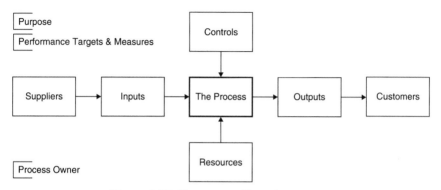

Figure 2.28 The composition of a process

A brief explanation of each process component is given below:

- **Purpose**. A short description of what the process is intended to achieve, i.e. what value it is adding to the business.
- **Performance Targets and Measures**. These are the predetermined performance levels you decide and the tangible metrics that are used to prove the process is performing. More details on this can be found in Section 10.2.
- **Process Owner**. Every process should have one designated owner who is accountable for its execution.
- **Suppliers**. Consider this the source of inputs to a process. It could be another department or another process.
- **Input**. Those items needed to produce the outputs. They should not be confused with the resources needed to perform the process. For example a set of accounts could be the input needed for performing a financial analysis process.
- **Controls**. Those standards defined by yourself (or possibly legislation) that impacts upon the way a process is performed.
- **Resources**. These can be:
  - **Personnel**. Define who is responsible for carrying out the process.
  - **Infrastructure**. Any equipment required to perform the process to an acceptable level.
  - **Support Systems**. These could be computer software packages that have to be used to perform a specific activity.
- **Outputs**. The expected deliverable from a process. This may form the input to another process, but in all instances it will add value to a business.
- **Customers**. Ultimately all processes deliver something (the output) to a customer. Now that could be the ultimate purchaser of a product or service or someone internal to your business, such as a stores controller taking delivery of equipment from goods inward.

All the above points should be considered before embarking upon drawing up a process.

In ISO 9001:2000, Core Business and supporting processes are used in an identical way to define how resources and activities are combined, controlled and converted into deliverables. Processes are the key to providing a clear understanding of what an organisation does and the quality controls it has in place to do those activities.

These processes are explained in more detail on the following pages.

2.6.2 Core Business Process

The Core Business Process describes the end to end activities involved in producing a contract deliverable be it something tangible (e.g. a car) or a

Table 2.1 Core Business and supporting processes

Core Business Process	Describes the end to end activities involved in an organisation manufacturing or supplying a deliverable. These activities which, when combined into a logical sequence, takes you from receipt of an order (or marketing opportunity) through to the realisation of the finished product or service.
Secondary Supporting Process	Those activities that are vital to attaining the desired levels of quality but which are seen as supporting the core business process.

service. It commences with the definition of corporate policy and ends when the product is manufactured and/or marketed.

A process owner with full responsibility and authority for managing the process and achieving process objectives should be nominated. For the core business process this would generally be the company Director.

2.6.3 Supporting processes

The Core Business Process is then supplemented by a number of supporting processes that describe the infrastructure required to manufacture (or supply) the product on time.

A flowchart of a typical supporting process is shown in Figure 2.30. Ownership of supporting processes generally falls to functional heads.

Of course the only way for an organisation to ensure repeat orders is to control quality. Consequently, it is essential that you define your quality policy and objectives for each supporting process.

Thus, for each process within the flowchart there will be accompanying documentation detailing:

- **Objective** – what the process aims to achieve.
- **Scope** – what the process covers.
- **Responsible owner** – who is ultimately responsible for implementing the process.
- **Policy** – what the organisation intends doing to ensure quality is controlled.
- **Key performance indicators** – those items of objective evidence that can be used as a way of monitoring performance of the process.
- reference to **supporting system documentation** (i.e. QPs and WIs).

Supporting processes run in parallel with the core business process, and are equally important as they control all other activities that may influence the quality of the product.

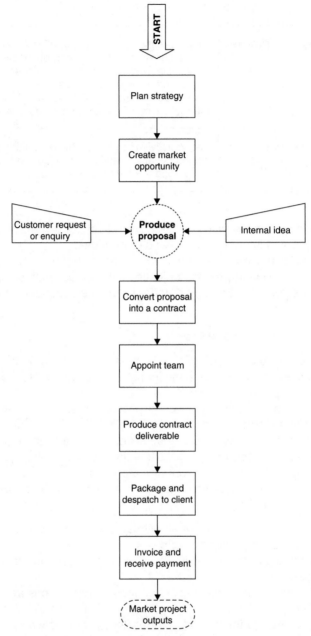

Figure 2.29 An example Core Business Process

Supporting processes may include such things as:

- identification, provision of suitable staff;
- management and support of staff;
- identification and provision of information;

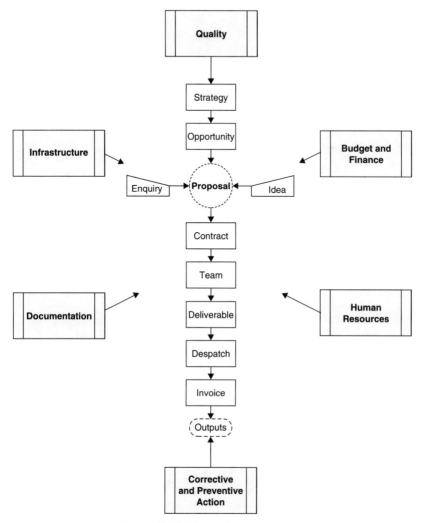

Figure 2.30 Supporting processes

- identification and provision of materials;
- identification and provision of equipment and facilities;
- management of the QMS;
- continual improvement.

The purpose of supporting processes is to document those activities that are essential for supporting and achieving the core business process.

Further examples of supporting processes are shown in Figures 2.31 and 2.32.

These supporting processes will have an identical structure to the core process, and will also have their own associated supporting documentation (i.e. QPs and WIs).

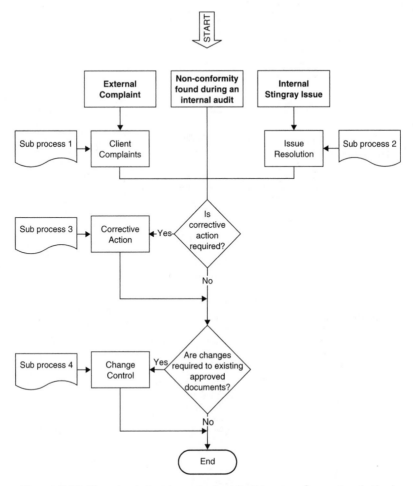

Figure 2.31 Flowchart showing a typical (in this case Corrective Action) supporting process

2.6.4 Inter-relationship of process documentation

Most processes are documented to give a complete picture of how to perform the activity to a consistent level of quality. The level of detail varies depending whether it is a:

- **Process Map** – a pictorial representation of activities which make up a process.
- **Quality Procedure** – an enlargement of the process explaining how it is controlled; its objective, scope and key performance indicators;
- **Work Instruction** – the 'fine print' required to perform a specific activity.

All these documents are explained in more detail elsewhere in this book.

Identification, provision, management and support of staff

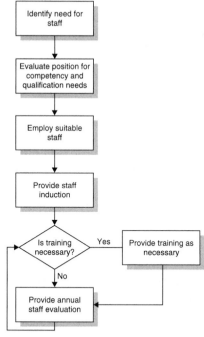

Figure 2.32 Another example of a supporting process flowchart

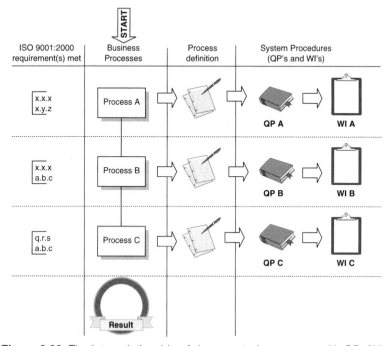

Figure 2.33 The inter-relationship of documented processes with QPs/WIs.
NOTE: By using a matrix such as this, it is possible to identify the parts of
ISO 9001:2000 which are met by each process.

2.6.5 The hierarchy of processes

When developing process maps they can become very complex. It is therefore recommended that you develop a hierarchy of process maps, which enables users to 'drill down' through a number of levels to reach the desired level of detail.

Figure 2.34 shows one way in which this can be achieved. Level 1 (The Overview) does nothing but show a summary of the core business process and the supporting processes. Should you wish to know more detail on a certain process, then by drilling down to the Level 2 maps you can get more information on the activities making up that specific process. If more detail is required then further levels can be added as shown, until you perhaps choose to supplement the maps with a written procedure.

This type of hierarchy is ideal for producing computer based management systems, where the functionality offered by websites enables process maps to be linked, thereby simplifying navigation between maps. Further details on using computer technology to enhance your managements system can be found in Chapter 11.

2.7 What is a Quality Procedure?

Procedure – 'Specified way to carry out an activity or a process'
(ISO 9000:2000)

Quality Procedures (QPs) are used to implement the core and supporting processes of an organisation. QPs detail **what** has to be carried out to meet the requirements of these processes and their associated Quality Policies. Without procedures an organisation's best intentions will not always be met.

Think of QPs as clear concise instructions. For example, management decrees that all problems found within the organisation must go through a problem-solving process (i.e. management sets a policy). A member of staff couldn't be expected to know how to do this without clear instructions. Even worse, the entire work force would have their own ideas about solving problems and further problems would arise because of this.

It is, therefore, essential that all QPs are written down so that everyone knows what to do.

Remember, however, that human nature puts us off reading text. So, for simpler procedures you may only need a process map. It is not mandatory to write procedures for everything.

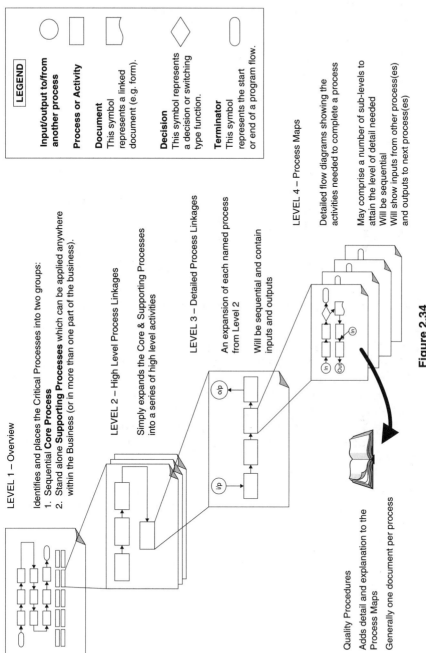

LEGEND

Input/output to/from another process

Process or Activity

Document
This symbol represents a linked document (e.g. form).

Decision
This symbol represents a decision or switching type function.

Terminator
This symbol represents the start or end of a program flow.

LEVEL 1 – Overview

Identifies and places the Critical Processes into two groups:
1. Sequential **Core Process**
2. Stand alone **Supporting Processes** which can be applied anywhere within the Business (or in more than one part of the business).

LEVEL 2 – High Level Process Linkages

Simply expands the Core & Supporting Processes into a series of high level activities

LEVEL 3 – Detailed Process Linkages

An expansion of each named process from Level 2

Will be sequential and contain inputs and outputs

LEVEL 4 – Process Maps

Detailed flow diagrams showing the activities needed to complete a process

May comprise a number of sub-levels to attain the level of detail needed
Will be sequential
Will show inputs from other process(es) and outputs to next process(es)

Quality Procedures

Adds detail and explanation to the Process Maps

Generally one document per process

Figure 2.34

Figure 2.35 Written procedures makes all the difference!

2.7.1 What is the best way to write a Quality Procedure

A simple rule is don't bother unless you really have to. A degree of common sense must prevail when writing procedures and due consideration must be given to the competency of the personnel performing them.

If you employ highly skilled professionals it would be foolish to spend hours writing a procedure on something for which they are already qualified to do or for which standards and guidelines already exist. For example, you would not tell a Civil Engineer how to design a bridge.

On the other hand you will probably want to write a procedure where you use untrained staff to perform it.

The old adage that a picture paints a thousand words stands true for QPs. No one likes reading and visually representing an organisation's QPs has always proved successful! If you can do without a written procedure, do so. Use a process map instead.

These easy-to-follow flowcharts can be enhanced with explanatory text so that the entire process is clearly understood and staff are easily trained. The benefit of flowcharts is that they can be stuck up on notice boards so that the people who have to implement the procedure can readily see what they are expected to do. Ideally they should be coloured for maximum effect.

2.7.2 What should go into a Quality Procedure?

QPs form the basic documentation used for planning and controlling all activities that impact on quality and add explanatory detail to Process

Maps. They detail how an organisation's policy is to be implemented by adding the meat to the process-specific policies. They should cover all the applicable elements of ISO 9001:2000 and detail procedures that concern the organisation's actual method of operation. These will normally remain relatively constant, regardless of the product, system or process being supplied.

Each QP should cover a specific part of the Core Business Process or one of its supporting processes, e.g., contract review, document control, audit procedures, training and should be easily traced back to the process-specific policies dictated by senior management.

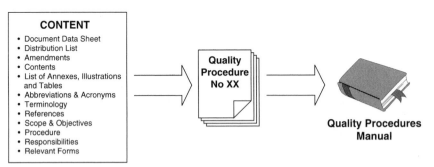

CONTENT
- Document Data Sheet
- Distribution List
- Amendments
- Contents
- List of Annexes, Illustrations and Tables
- Abbreviations & Acronyms
- Terminology
- References
- Scope & Objectives
- Procedure
- Responsibilities
- Relevant Forms

Quality Procedure No XX

Quality Procedures Manual

Figure 2.36 What goes into a Quality Procedure

QPs should not normally include technical requirements or specialist procedures required for the manufacture of a product or delivery of a system/service. These sorts of details are generally explained in Work Instructions (see Section 2.8 for further details). QPs can (and usually do) form a large bulk of the QMS.

The layout and format of QPs should be consistent so that staff can become accustomed to a familiar structure. This also helps to ensure systematic compliance with the ISO 9001:2000 standard.

QPs shall cover and include:

- **Document data sheet** – all the salient information about the document – file name, who wrote it, a summary of the contents, when it was approved, who approved it, etc.
- **Distribution list** – a record of everyone who has a controlled copy of the document.
- **Amendments** – a record of all changes made to the document.
- **Contents list** – a list of all the chapters, sections, parts and annexes, etc. that make up this document.
- **List of annexes** – all parts of a document should be traceable, especially when they are in separate volumes.
- **List of illustrations/tables** – a list of all the figures and tables included in the document.

- **Abbreviations and acronyms** – an explanation of any abbreviations or acronyms used in the document.
- **Terminology** – an explanation of any technical or confusing terminology used in the document.
- **References** – any reference material that is specifically referred to in the document.
- **Scope and objectives** – this should list why you need the procedure, what it is for, the area covered and any exclusions.
- **Procedure overview and procedure** – this is the main part of the document and details in clear, concise and unambiguous terms the actions and methods to be used. Ideally the procedure should be detailed in the same logical order as its associated process map.
- **Responsibilities** – clear specifications of who is responsible for implementing the procedure and who can carry it out including (if necessary), minimum training requirements.
- **Relevant forms** – the identification of any forms, paperwork or computerised forms required to implement the procedure.

A typical Quality Procedure is shown in Annex A to this Section. In this example, the QP relates to 'Issue Resolution' which can be traced back to clause 8.5 of ISO 9001:2000 (Improvement).

Explanatory calls out boxes (similar to the one shown below) have been added to the example to highlight important aspects of the QP.

> This is a call out box. Keep an eye out for them in the following Annex.

Figure 2.37 A sample call out box to be found in Annex A

2.7.3 Annex A – Example Quality Procedure

Quality Procedure No. 2

Issue Resolution

Version Number: 01.00

File Name: S-QMS-002

Document Data Sheet

This page carries all the salient information on the document

Title	This version	Date
Quality Procedure No. 2 – Issue Resolution	**01.00**	**17.12.00**
	File Number	No of pages
	S-QMS-002	**12**

Author(s)

R L Tricker

Subject

Stingray Quality Management System

Executive Summary

It is essential that all issues (whether technical, management, quality, financial or other), that can have an effect on the overall efficiency of Stingray are first identified and recorded. Once this has been done they can be assessed by the manager directly responsible and referred to the appropriate management level for resolution.

Issues can be originated:
- by an individual on a contract (e.g. a consultant);
- by an individual within a department (e.g. a secretary);
- as a result of a contract, departmental or Stingray management meeting;
- as the result of contractual work.

This summary provides the details of the scope covered by the QP.

Stingray staff may raise an issue **at any time.**

This Quality Procedure is mandatory and applies to everyone in Stingray and shall be used for any issue that can have an effect on a contract.

Keywords

Activity, Deliverable, Document, Internal Audit, Issue, Issue Resolution, Issue Resolution Form, Quality Procedure, Report, Responsible Manager, Work Instruction.

Approved

....   **Date: ....**
(Managing Director)

Section 4.2.3(a) requires management to: *'approve documents for adequacy prior to issue'.*

Distribution List (controlled copies)

1. Managing Director
2. General Manager
3. Organisation Secretary
4. Technical Manager
5. Quality Manager
6. Administration Office
7. Spare copy (1)
8. Spare copy (2)

Section 5.5.6(d) requires *'that relevant versions of applicable documents are available at points of use'*.

Note: As computers become part of every company's business (and saving paper as environmental constraints are becoming more of a requirement) quite often only an electronic version of the QMS exists. This version is controlled by the Quality Manager who is responsible for keeping it up to date. Staff can take copies of the server (or company's electronic filing system) in the knowledge that extracted copies are the most up to date. If sections of the QMS are being quoted in contracts the Project Manager concerned will have to liaise with the Quality Manager to ensure that the latest copy is used.

Amendments

Amendment number	Amendment details	Author	Date (dd.mm.yy)
00.01	Draft Version 1	RLT	18.08.00
00.02	Draft Version 2	RLT	25.08.00
00.03	Draft Version 3	RLT	08.09.00
00.04	Draft Version 4	RLT	04.12.00
01.00	First Issue	RLT	17.12.00

Clause 4.2.3(c) states the requirement *'to identify the current revision status of documents'*

This table allows these changes to be recorded.

Contents

List of Annexes

Annex	Title	File Name (if separate document)
1	Issue Resolution Form	
2	Issue Resolution Log	

All parts of a document should be traceable, especially when they are separate volumes.

List of Illustrations

Flowchart for Issue Resolution

List of Tables

Nil.

Abbreviations and Acronyms

Abbreviation	Definition
Stingray	Stingray Management Consultants
QP	Quality Procedure
WI	Work Instruction

Terminology

> Any industry-specific or confusing terms should be explained for the benefit of the reader.

Term	Definition
Activity	May concern a contract or venture undertaken by Stingray staff as instructed by Stingray management.
Deliverable	The work produced as a result of a contract or activity.
Document	Includes all Stingray reports, deliverables, and official documents, both hard and soft copies.
Stingray staff	Any individual contracted to work for Stingray.
Issue	Any technical, managerial, financial or other situation/detail that can affect a contract, whether it is beneficial or not.
Report	The result of a Stingray contract, sometimes referred to as a 'deliverable'.
Resolution	The culmination and solution to a raised Issue.
Responsible Manager	The appropriate Stingray Manager or Director.

References

> Material associated or referenced in the document.

Abbreviation	Title	Version	Issue date
WI/06	Issue Resolution Forms	01.00	17.12.00

> For your convenience, this WI has been included as an example at Annex B to Section 2.8, page 61.

1 Scope and objectives

1.1 Introduction

It is essential that all issues (whether technical, management, quality, financial or other), that can have an effect on the overall efficiency of Stingray are first identified and recorded. Once this has been done they can be assessed by the manager directly responsible and then referred to the appropriate management level for resolution.

Issues can be originated:

- by an individual on a contract (e.g. a consultant);
- by an individual within a department (e.g. a secretary);
- as a result of a contract, departmental or Stingray management meeting;
- as the result of contractual work.

Stingray staff may raise an issue at any time.

1.2 Purpose

To provide a process for the resolution of issues.

> A clear indication of why the QP is needed, what it is for and the area it covers.

1.3 Scope

This Quality Procedure is mandatory and applies to all Stingray contracts and shall be used for any issue that can have an effect on a contract and/or contract deliverable.

This Quality Procedure will also be used where the resolution of an issue is already known, so that the resolution can be disseminated to other interested parties.

Even if the resolution to an issue is patently obvious or has already been addressed, it is essential that all issues are raised and processed according to this Quality Procedure.

General comment – the 'do nothing' option is normally taken as unacceptable but it is still given consideration and recommended where it is the only viable solution.

2 Procedure overview

The procedure is summarised below and detailed in the process map in Figure 1.

1. Identify issue;
2. Record and log issue;
3. Check issue;
4. Enter details in Issue Resolution Log;
5. Identify all possible options;
6. Analyse options and recommendations;
7. Assess results of action taken;
8. Record and log decision;
9. Issue closure.

The following section of this example QP lays down the 'controlled conditions' (i.e. the procedure or process) for resolving issues which, if not addressed, would comprise the quality of a contract (Section 7.3.4 Design and development review).

This QP will also be of use in complying with

- Section 8.5.3, as it is a means of identifying and implementing preventive action;
- Section 8.2.2, as it will provide the auditable proof that the organisation is implementing preventive action.

3 Procedure

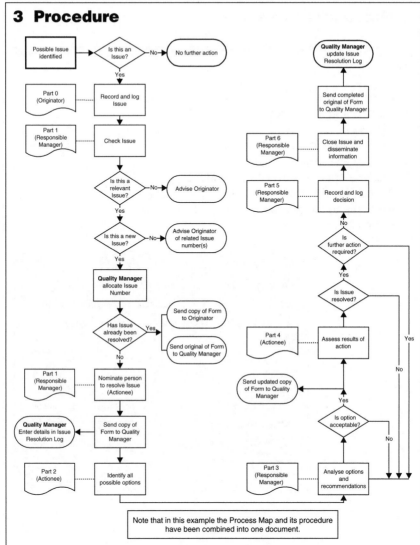

Note that in this example the Process Map and its procedure have been combined into one document.

Figure 1 Process Map for Issue Resolution

3.1 Identify issue

Stingray staff may raise an issue **at any time**.

It is important that all issues are raised, however trivial. Even if the issue has already been resolved or is capable of being resolved by the originator, it must still be raised and addressed using this Issue Resolution Quality Procedure, as the issue may be of use to other parties. This procedure shall also ensure that the resolution of issues is traceable.

3.2 Issue Resolution Form

Once an Issue Resolution Form has been raised by the originator (see Annex 1 and WI/6 – Issue Resolution Forms), the form is passed on to the Responsible Manager who shall check whether it is a relevant, new or related issue.

If this is a new issue, the Responsible Manager shall obtain a new issue number from the Quality Manager and appoint an Actionee to resolve the issue. He shall also send an information copy of the form to the Quality Manager. The Actionee shall identify all possible options after which the Responsible Manager shall review and discuss these options with the Actionee before deciding upon the most appropriate action.

Once the Actionee has completed the issue resolution and is satisfied that the issue has been resolved, the Issue Resolution Form is completed and the information disseminated by the Responsible Manager. A copy of the completed form shall be sent to the Quality Manager.

3.3 Issue Resolution Log

The Issue Resolution Log (see Annex 2) is maintained by the Quality Manager.

The Quality Manager shall review the Issue Resolution Log on a regular basis and discuss any problems which may arise as a result of an issue raised and ensure that issues are dealt with in a timely fashion.

4 Responsibilities

4.1 Stingray staff

All Stingray staff are responsible for identifying and recording issues (e.g. financial, technical, managerial or quality related) and for bringing them to the attention of the Stingray management.

4.2 Responsible Managers

Responsible Managers are responsible for:

- checking all new issues;
- delegating the investigation to an appropriate person;
- reviewing the Actionee's recommended solutions and selecting the most appropriate option;
- evaluating the resolution of the issue;
- closing the issue.

4.3 Actionee

The Actionee (i.e. the person nominated to investigate the issue) is responsible for:

- identifying all possible options and providing a recommended solution;
- resolving the issue (when requested by the Responsible Manager).

4.4 Quality Manager

The Quality Manager is responsible for:

- the issue and control of this Quality Procedure;
- ensuring that it is regularly reviewed and updated;
- allocating new Issue Numbers;
- maintaining the Issue Resolution Log;
- maintaining a database of Keywords and previously resolved issues;
- ensuring that regular internal quality audits that address the continued applicability of this procedure are scheduled and completed.

Annex 1 – Issue Resolution Form

Department:		Issue No:	

Part 0: Record and Log Issue (to be completed by the Originator)

Raised by:		Date:	
Target resolution date:		Priority:	

Description of Issue:

Possible consequences:

Supporting documentation attached: **YES/NO**   Continued: **YES/NO**

Part 1: Check Issue (to be completed by the Responsible Manager)

Is this a new Issue: YES/NO

If NO:

Related Issue number(s):	
Key words:	

If YES:

Actionee:	

Date actioned/allocated task:		Target completion date:	

Details entered in Issue Resolution Log: YES/NO

Key words:

Remarks:

Part 2: Identify All possible options (to be completed by the Actionee)

Option(s):

Part 2 (cont):

Recommended option(s):

Affects:

Supporting documentation: YES/NO

Options assessment required: YES/NO

Part 3: Analyse options and recommendations (to be completed by the Responsible Manager)

Agreed option:

Target date:

Part 4: Assess results of action (to be completed by the Actionee)

Assessment:

Recommended further action:

Recommended distribution:

Part 5: Record and log decision (to be completed by the Responsible Manager)

Has the Issue been satisfactorily resolved: YES/NO

If 'NO', details of further action required:

Outcome:

Part 6: Issue Closure (to be completed by the Responsible Manager)

Signature:		**Date:**	

Dissemination of Information:

Annex 2 – Issue Resolution Log

Issue No	Description of Issue	Date Raised	Raised By	Priority	Actionee	Target Date	Date Closed

2.8 What is a Work Instruction?

A Work Instructions (WIs) provides the 'nitty gritty' detail required to carry out a specific job in an exact manner and to a predetermined standard. They detail how an organisation manufactures a product or supplies a service, and the controls that it has in place to ensure the quality of that product is consistent.

Figure 2.38 Written instructions should leave no room for error

WIs describe, in detail, procedures such as 'what is to be done', 'who should do it', 'when it should be done', 'what supplies, services and equipment are to be used' and 'what criteria have to be satisfied'. These WIs should be regularly reviewed for their continuing acceptability, validity and effectiveness.

Inferior or poor design, ambiguous specifications, incomplete or inaccurate WIs and methods, non-conformance etc. are the most frequent causes of defects during manufacture or the delivery of a service. In order that management can be sure that everything is being carried out under the strictest of controlled conditions, it is crucial that all WIs (in fact any written instruction) are clear, accurate and fully documented.

Good WIs avoid confusion, show exactly what work has to be done or what services are to be provided. They also delegate authority and responsibility.

Without a written guide, different interpretations in policies and procedures can easily arise and these variations can result in confusion and uncertainty.

As BSI reminds us, *'Instructions provide direction to various levels of personnel. They also provide criteria for assessing the effectiveness of control and the quality of the material, ensure uniformity of understanding, performance and continuity when personnel changes occur. They provide the basis for control, evaluation and review.'*

2.8.1 What should go into a Work Instruction?

In summary a WI should, as a minimum, contain:

- **Document data sheet** – all the salient information about the document – file name, who wrote it, a summary of the contents, when it was approved, who approved it, etc.

- **Distribution list** – a record of everyone who has a controlled copy of the document.
- **Amendments** – a record of all changes made to the document.
- **Contents list** – a list of all the chapters, sections, parts and annexes etc. making up this document.
- **List of annexes** – all parts of a document should be traceable, especially when they are in separate volumes.
- **List of illustrations/tables** – a list of all the figures and tables included in the document.
- **Abbreviations and Acronyms** – an explanation of any abbreviations or acronyms used in the document.
- **Terminology** – an explanation of any technical or confusing terminology used in the document.
- **References** – any reference material that is specifically referred to in the document.
- **Scope and objectives** – this should define exactly what the WI is needed for. Normally this is a very simple statement because a Work Instruction would normally be limited to one process (e.g. this Work Instruction details the actions to be taken to dig a square hole).
- **Procedure** – this will state the manner of production, installation or application where the absence of such controls would adversely affect quality (e.g. the hole shall be dug using hand shovels only and be temporarily shored to prevent collapse). Consideration should also be given to any safety implications that may exist when carrying out the process;
- **Responsibility** – the WI must clearly state who can carry out the process;

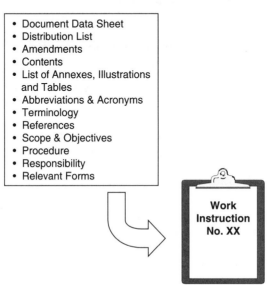

Figure 2.39 What goes into a Work Instruction?

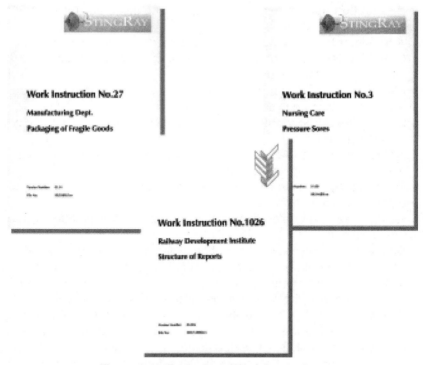

Figure 2.40 Examples of Work Instructions

- **Relevant forms** – the identification of forms, paperwork or computerised forms required to implement the WI.

2.8.2 How many Work Instructions can I have?

The manufacture of a device or the delivery of a process or service may require the completion of more than one WI. It is perfectly acceptable, indeed desirable, to separate processes into a number of WIs because:

- it would be very difficult to write a single WI for large items, such as manufacturing an aircraft or laying on the catering services for the Royal Tournament;
- each WI may require staff with different levels of training and qualifications;
- a particular contract may only require the completion of certain WIs;
- small concise WIs are more easily revised.

A typical WI is shown in Annex B to this section.

2.8.3 Annex B – Example Work Instruction

Work Instruction No. 6

Issue Resolution Forms

Version Number:　01.00

File Name:　　　S-QMS-004

Document Data Sheet

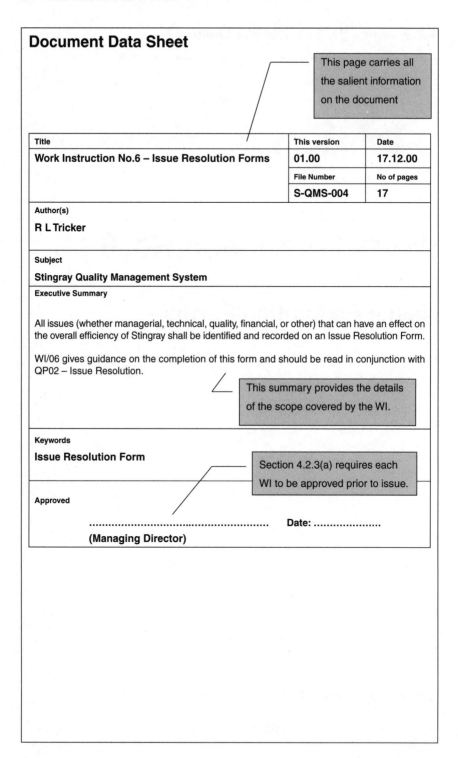

This page carries all the salient information on the document

Title	This version	Date
Work Instruction No.6 – Issue Resolution Forms	**01.00**	**17.12.00**
	File Number	**No of pages**
	S-QMS-004	**17**

Author(s)

R L Tricker

Subject

Stingray Quality Management System

Executive Summary

All issues (whether managerial, technical, quality, financial, or other) that can have an effect on the overall efficiency of Stingray shall be identified and recorded on an Issue Resolution Form.

WI/06 gives guidance on the completion of this form and should be read in conjunction with QP02 – Issue Resolution.

This summary provides the details of the scope covered by the WI.

Keywords

Issue Resolution Form

Section 4.2.3(a) requires each WI to be approved prior to issue.

Approved

....   **Date:** ....
(Managing Director)

Distribution List (controlled copies)

1. Managing Director

2. General Manager

3. Organisation Secretary

4. Technical Manager

5. Quality Manager

6. Administration Office

7. Spare copy (1)

8. Spare copy (2)

Section 4.2.3(d) requires *'that relevant versions of applicable documents are available at points of use'.*

Amendments

Amendment number	Amendment details	Author	Date (dd.mm.yy)
00.01	Draft Version 1	RLT	18.08.00
00.02	Draft Version 2	RLT	25.08.00
00.03	Draft Version 3	RLT	08.09.00
00.04	Draft Version 4	RLT	04.12.00
01.00	First Issue	RLT	17.12.00

Section 4.2.3(c) states the requirement *'to identify the current revision status of documents'*

This table allows these changes to be recorded.

Contents

Document Data Sheet
Distribution List (controlled copies)
Amendments
Contents
List of Annexes
Abbreviations and Acronyms
Terminology
References
1　Scope and objectives
2　Procedure – completing the Issue Resolution Form
　2.1　Record and log Issue – Part 0
　2.2　Check issue – Part 1
　2.3　Identify all possible options – Part 2
　2.4　Analyse options and recommendations – Part 3
　2.5　Assess results of action taken – Part 4
　2.6　Record and log decision – Part 5
　2.7　Issue closure – Part 6
Annex 1 – Issue Resolution Form
Annex 2 – Issue Resolution Log

List of Annexes

Annex	Title	File Name (if separate document)
1	Issue Resolution Form	
2	Issue Resolution Log	

All parts of a document should be traceable, especially when they are separate volumes.

Abbreviations and Acronyms

Abbreviation	Definition
Stingray	Stingray Management Consultants
QP	Quality Procedure
WI	Work Instruction

Terminology

Any industry-specific or confusing terms should be explained for the benefit of the reader.

Term	Definition
Activity	May concern a contract or venture undertaken by Stingray staff as instructed by Stingray management.
Deliverable	The work produced as a result of a contract or activity.
Document	Includes all Stingray reports, deliverables, and official documents, both hard and soft copies.
Stingray staff	Any individual contracted to work for Stingray.
Issue	Any technical, managerial, financial or other situation/ detail that can affect a contract, whether it is beneficial or not.
Report	The result of a Stingray contract, sometimes referred to as a 'deliverable'.
Resolution	The culmination and solution to a raised Issue.
Responsible Manager	The appropriate Stingray Manager or Director.

References

Material associated or referenced in the document.

Abbreviation	Title	Version	Issue date
QP/2	Issue Resolution	01.00	17.12.00

For your convenience, this has been included as an example at Annex 1 to 2.7, page 74

1 Scope and objectives

All issues (whether managerial, technical, quality, financial, or other) that can have an effect on the overall efficiency of Stingray shall be identified and recorded on an Issue Resolution Form.

WI/6 gives guidance on the completion of this form and should be read in conjunction with QP/2 – Issue Resolution.

2 Procedure – completing the Issue Resolution Form

2.1 Record and log Issue – Part 0

Department:		Issue No:	
Part 0: Record Log Issue (to be completed by the Originator)			
Raised by:		Date:	
Target resolution date:		Priority:	
Description of Issue:			
Possible consequences:			
Supporting documentation attached: **YES/NO** Continued: **YES/NO**			

Part 0 of the Issue Resolution Form (Annex 1; page 74) shall be completed by the originator as follows:

- **Department:** The department to which the originator is attached.
- **Issue No:** To be completed by the Quality Manager once it has been established that this is a new issue (see paragraph 2.2 of this WI).
- **Raised by:** The name of the originator and his role/affiliation to the department or contract.
- **Date:** The date on which the issue was raised.
- **Target resolution date:** This is a target date (set by the originator) by which an issue should be resolved.
- **Priority:** Each issue shall be allocated (by the originator) one of the following priority categories:
  - **Low:** Resolution of the issue is desirable, but not essential at this time;
  - **Medium:** The issue must be resolved, but not immediately;

- **High:** This issue shall have a major impact on the project unless it is resolved immediately.
- **Description of Issue and possible consequences:** This must be a full description so as to enable all of the relevant parties to fully understand the issue. If necessary a continuation sheet may be used and supporting documentation can be attached to the form. If this occurs, a list of attachments, (including references if applicable), should be added to the 'Description' part and the relevant 'Yes/No' boxes crossed. The possible consequences of an issue (if known) should also be detailed.

2.2 Check issue – Part 1

Part 1: Check Issue (to be completed by the Responsible Manager)		
Is this a new Issue: YES/NO		
If NO:		
Related Issue number(s):		
Key words:		
If YES:		
Actionee:		
Date actioned/allocated task:		Target completion date:
Details entered in Issue Resolution Log: YES/NO		
Key words:		
Remarks:		

This part shall be completed by the Responsible Manager as follows:

- **Is this a relevant issue:** The Responsible Manager shall determine whether this is an existing or potential problem. If he considers that the issue requires further investigation he shall proceed to the next stage. If, however, he considers that this is not a relevant issue, he shall return the form to the originator together with a suitable explanation.
- **Is this a new Issue:** The Responsible Manager shall check whether the issue has been raised previously.

Where an issue has been raised previously then the Responsible Manager shall enter details of the **Related Issue** (Resolution Form)

number(s) and any relevant **Keywords** and return the updated Issue Resolution Form to the originator with any relevant information.

If this is a new issue it shall be allocated an Issue Number (which shall be placed at the top of the Issue Resolution Form) by the Quality Manager.

The Quality Manager shall record the details in the in the Issue Resolution Log (Annex 2; page 76) which shall be maintained by him.

The Responsible Manager shall complete the remainder of this part of the form as follows:

- **Actionee:** The Responsible Manager shall decide on an appropriate person to resolve the issue.
- **Date actioned/allocated task:** The date on which the person was actioned (or allocated) to complete the task.
- **Target completion date:** This is normally the target date set by the originator (see Part 0) by which the issue should be resolved. If there is a difference between the dates then an appropriate note should be included in the **Remarks** part of this part.
- **Details entered in Issue Resolution Log:** This is a check (reminder) that the issue has been appropriately recorded for future reference by the Quality Manager.
- **Keywords:** The appropriate key words about the issue shall be entered here.
- **Remarks:** If the issue has already been resolved and the form has been raised to ensure its dissemination to other parties, the Responsible Manager makes the appropriate note in this part and returns it to the originator with instructions on how best to dissemi- nate the information. Reasons for allocating this task a different **Target completion date** may also be recorded here.

An information copy of the Issue Resolution Form shall be sent to the Quality Manager.

2.3 Identify all possible options – Part 2

Part 2: Identify All possible options (to be completed by the Actionee)

Option(s):
Option(s) recommended:
Effects:
Supporting documentation: **YES/NO** Options assessment required: **YES/NO**

Part 2 shall be completed by the Actionee to resolve the issue.

The Responsible Manager shall task the Actionee with finding all possible options to resolve the specific issue together with an indication of their relative merits.

The Actionee shall identify the possible options to resolve the issue. (It may be necessary for the Actionee to research the issue in order to generate a number of options.) The Actionee then completes Part 2 as follows:

- **Option(s):** This must be a complete listing of all possible options that are available to resolve the issue.
- **Option(s) recommended:** The Actionee's recommended option(s) to resolve the issue.
- **Effects:** Complete details of all the effects caused by implementing the option(s) to resolve the issue. This may possibly include a list of documents, Process Maps, Quality Procedures or Work Instructions that need to be altered, reports that need to be updated or deliverables that require amendment, etc.
- **Supporting documentation:** An indicator to show that supporting documentation has been attached to the Issue Resolution Form.
- **Option assessment required:** To show whether further evaluation of the option(s) is required.

2.4 Analyse options and recommendations – Part 3

> **Part 3: Analyse options and recommendations** (to be completed by the Responsible Manager)
>
> > **Agreed option:**
> >
> > **Target date:**

The Responsible Manager completes Part 3 as follows:

- **Agreed option:** The Responsible Manager shall review and discuss all the possible options with the Actionee and select the most appropriate option. The Actionee is responsible for carrying out the action to resolve the issue, whether directly or indirectly through delegation.
- The Responsible Manager shall use the criteria developed at this stage as the basis for the later decision as to whether or not the issue has been fully resolved. It is essential, therefore, that both parties fully understand what is required.
- **Target date:** The date (set by the Responsible Manager) for completion of the action to resolve the issue.

2.5 Assess results of action taken – Part 4

Part 4: Assess results of action (to be completed by the Actionee)

Assessment:

Recommended further action:

Recommended distribution:

When the Actionee is satisfied that the issue is resolved and all necessary actions have been carried out, he completes Part 4 of the Issue Resolution Form as follows:

- **Assessment:** This part should be used to briefly describe how the issue has been resolved. If attachments are supplied, these should be listed in this part (including references if applicable). This part should also include the rationale for the chosen option and a list of the outputs produced as a result of resolving the issue.
- **Recommended further action:** Details of any further or future actions that are required in order to finalise this issue.
- **Recommended distribution:** The Actionee may, where appropriate, recommend to whom the issue should be distributed.

2.6 Record and log decision – Part 5

Part 5: Record and log decision (to be completed by the Responsible Manager)

Has the issue been satisfactorily resolved: YES/NO

If 'NO', details of further action required:

Outcome:

The Responsible Manager shall complete Part 5 as follows:

- **Has issue been satisfactorily resolved Yes/No:** The Responsible Manager shall make a judgement as to whether or not the issue has been satisfactorily resolved.
- **If 'No' – Details of further action required:** If it is decided that the issue is not satisfactorily resolved then the relevant points shall be discussed with the Actionee to assess what further action needs to be taken in order to resolve the issue.
- **Outcome:** The details of the decision shall be filled in on the Issue Resolution Form on completion of the action. If completion is satisfactory then it can be signed off.

2.7 Issue closure – Part 6

Part 6: Issue Closure (to be completed by the Responsible Manager)			
Signature:		Date:	
Dissemination of Information:			

The Responsible Manager shall complete Part 6 as follows:

- **Signature and Date:** When the Responsible Manager is satisfied that the issue is completed satisfactorily, it shall be signed off. The Responsible Manager shall sign and date the Issue Resolution Form in Part 6 to indicate that the issue is now closed.
- **Dissemination of the decision:** The decision shall be disseminated to members of the sector and any other relevant parties.

The Responsible Manager shall send the completed Issue Resolution Form, plus any attachments, to the Quality Manager.

The Quality Manager shall complete the Date Closed in the Issue Resolution Log. The original of the Issue Resolution Form shall then be filed in the Issue Resolution Log and the copy of the form already in the log shall be destroyed.

Annex 1 – Issue Resolution Form

Department:		Issue No:	

Part 0: Record and Log Issue (to be completed by the Originator)

Raised by:		Date:	
Target resolution date:		Priority:	

Description of Issue:

Possible consequences:

Supporting documentation attached: **YES/NO**   Continued: **YES/NO**

Part 1: Check Issue (to be completed by the Responsible Manager)

Is this a new Issue: YES/NO

If NO:

Related Issue number(s):	
Key words:	

If YES:

Actionee:	
Date actioned/allocated task:		Target completion date:	

Details entered in Issue Resolution Log: YES/NO

Key words:

Remarks:

Part 2 : Identify All possible options (to be completed by the Actionee)

Option(s):

Part 2 (cont):

Recommended option(s):

Affects:

Supporting documentation: YES/NO

Options assessment required: YES/NO

Part 3: Analyse options and recommendations (to be completed by the Responsible Manager)

Agreed option:

Target date:

Part 4: Assess results of action (to be completed by the Actionee)

Assessment:

Recommended further action:

Recommended distribution:

Part 5: Record and log decision (to be completed by the Responsible Manager)

Has the Issue been satisfactorily resolved: YES/NO

If 'NO', details of further action required:

Outcome:

Part 6: Issue Closure (to be completed by the Responsible Manager)

Signature:		**Date:**	

Dissemination of Information:

Annex 2 – Issue Resolution Log

Issue No	Description of Issue	Date Raised	Raised By	Priority	Actionee	Target Date	Date Closed

2.9 What is a Quality Plan?

'... a document specifying which procedures and associated resources shall be applied, by whom and when to a specific project product, process or contract' (ISO 9000:2000)

Quality Plans are used to record the quality requirements for a particular contract, product or service and to monitor and assess adherence to those requirements.

You may already have quality controls for your normal products or services, but what do you do if someone wants something different? You could simply apply your existing quality controls, but it is unlikely that they will cover all eventualities. What you need is a Quality Plan to address the specific requirements of that particular contract.

A Quality Plan is effectively a sub-set of the actual Quality Manual. Some may even say that it is a 'customised Quality Manual' as the layout of the Quality Plan will be very similar to that of the Quality Manual and need only **refer** to the Process Maps, QPs and WIs contained in that Quality Manual. These will be supplemented by detailed **contract-specific** Process Maps, QPs and WIs.

In essence, Quality Plans provide a collated summary of the requirements for a specific project. They will cover all of the quality practices and resources that are going to be used, the sequence of events relevant to that product, the specific allocation of responsibilities, methods, QPs and WIs, together with details of the testing, inspection, examination and audit programme stages.

In addition to being ideal for controlling the quality of manufactured goods, Quality Plans are equally suited to the delivery of services. For example, your organisation may provide catering services, in which case Quality Plans would be an ideal way of controlling wedding receptions etc., because no two events are the same.

The main requirement of a Quality Plan, however, is to provide the customer (and the workforce) with clear, concise instructions. These instructions must be adequately recorded and be made available for examination by the customer. They must leave no room for error but equally they should be flexible and written in such a way that it is possible to modify their content to reflect changing circumstances.

A well thought out Quality Plan will divide the project into stages, show what type of inspection has to be completed at the beginning, during, or end of each stage and indicate how these details should be recorded. The Quality Plan should be planned and developed in conjunction with design, development, manufacturing, subcontract pre and post installation work and ensure that all functions have been fully catered for.

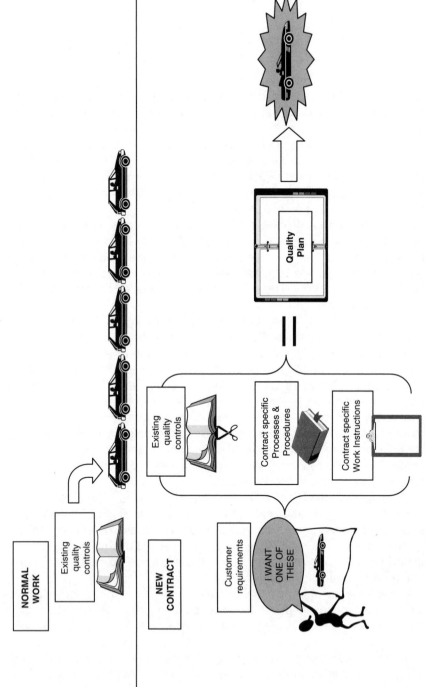

Figure 2.41 Quality Plans are needed to control the quality of specific projects

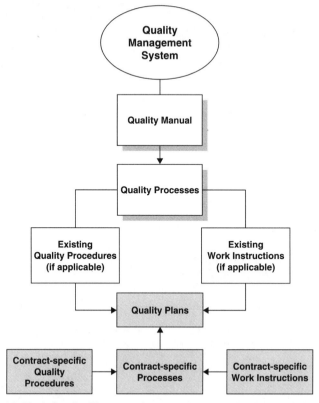

Figure 2.42 A Quality Plan supplements the organisation's existing QMS

Figure 2.43 The lack of a Quality Plan can have disastrous results!

2.9.1 What should be covered by a Quality Plan?

One of the main objectives of quality planning is to identify any special or unusual requirements, processes and techniques (including those requirements that are unusual by reason of newness, unfamiliarity, lack of experience and/or absence of precedents). As ISO 9000 points out, if the contract specifies that a Quality Plan is required, then that Quality Plan should fully cover the areas listed in Figure 2.44.

2.9.1.1 Management responsibility

The Quality Plan should show who is responsible for:

- ensuring activities are planned, implemented, controlled and monitored;
- communicating requirements and resolving problems;
- reviewing audit results;
- authorising exemption requests;
- implementing corrective action requests.

Figure 2.44 What should be covered by a Quality Plan

Where the necessary documentation is already available under an existing QMS, the Quality Plan need only refer to a specific situation or specification.

Quality Plans, by their very nature vary considerably depending upon the product/service being provided. However, in general they should cover:

2.9.1.2 Contract review

Contract review should cover:

- when, how and by whom the review is made;
- how the results are to be documented;
- how conflicting instructions or ambiguities are resolved.

2.9.1.3 Design control

Design control should indicate:

- when, how and by whom the design process, validation and verification of the design output is carried out, controlled and documented;
- any customer involvement;
- applicable codes of practice, standards, specifications and regulatory requirements.

2.9.1.4 Document and data control

Document and data control should refer to:

- what is provided and how it is controlled;
- how related documents will be identified;
- how and by whom access to the documents can be obtained;
- how and by whom the original documents are reviewed and approved.

2.9.1.5 Purchasing

Under the heading of purchasing the following should be indicated:

- the important products to be purchased;
- the source and requirements relating to them;
- the method, evaluation, selection and control of subcontractors;
- the need for a subcontractor's Quality Plan in order to satisfy the regulatory requirements applicable to purchase of products/services.

2.9.1.6 Customer supplied product

Customer supplied products should refer to:

- how they are identified and controlled;
- how they are verified as meeting specified requirements;
- how non-conformance is dealt with.

2.9.1.7 Product identification and traceability

If traceability is a requirement then the plan should:

- define its scope and extent (including how services/products are identified);
- indicate how contractual and regulatory authority traceability requirements are identified and incorporated into working documents;
- indicate how records are to be generated, controlled and distributed.

2.9.1.8 Process control

Process control may include:

- the contract-specific processes, QPs and WIs;
- process steps;
- methods to monitor and control processes;
- service/product characteristics;
- reference criteria for workmanship;
- special and qualified processes;
- tools, techniques and methods to be used.

2.9.1.9 Inspection and testing

Inspection and testing should indicate:

- any inspection and test plan;
- how the product shall be verified;
- the location of inspection and test points;
- procedures and acceptance criteria;
- witness verification points (customers as well as regulatory);
- where, when and how the customer requires third parties to perform:
  - type tests;
  - witness testing;
  - service/product verification;
  - material, service/product, process or personnel certification.

2.9.1.10 Inspection, measuring and test equipment

Inspection, measuring and test equipment should:

- refer to the identity of the equipment;
- refer to the method of calibration;
- indicate and record calibration status and usage of the equipment;
- indicate specific requirements for the identification of inspection and test status.

2.9.1.11 Non-conforming product

Under the heading of non-conforming service/product, an indication should be given:

- of how such a service/product is identified and segregated;
- the degree or type of rework allowed;
- the circumstances under which the supplier can request concessions.

Details should also be provided with respect to:

- corrective and preventive action;
- handling, storage, packaging, preservation and delivery.

2.9.2 Other considerations

Quality Plans should:

- indicate key quality records (i.e. what they are, how long they should be kept, where and by whom);
- suggest how legal or regulatory requirements are to be satisfied;
- specify the form in which records should be kept (e.g. paper, microfilm or disc);
- define liability, storage, retrievability, disposition and confidentiality requirements;
- include the nature and extent of quality audits to be undertaken;
- indicate how the audit results are to be used to correct and prevent recurrence of deficiencies;
- show how the training of staff in new or revised operating methods is to be completed.

Where servicing is a specified requirement, suppliers should state their intentions to assure conformance to applicable servicing requirements, such as:

- regulatory and legislative requirements;
- industry codes and practices;
- service level agreements;
- training of customer personnel;
- availability of initial and ongoing support during the agreed time-period;
- statistical techniques, where relevant.

Note: ISO 10005 (Quality Management – Guidelines for Quality Plans) provides useful guidance on how to produce Quality Plans as well as including helpful suggestions on how to maintain an organisation's quality activities.

3 THE HISTORY OF QUALITY STANDARDS

Quality used to be about making sure that the product was right and with an emphasis on the manufacturer being required to produce something that could be inspected against a specific dimension or criterion. The product was then considered acceptable, or had to be reworked to become acceptable, or had to be scrapped (which could be very expensive). When things went wrong it was usual to blame the craftsmen (e.g. welders, painters, typists, etc.)!

Figure 3.1 Old fashioned Quality Control!

In the 1920s, a Munitions Standard was developed by the UK Ordnance Board to guarantee that bullets used during World War I were good (and safe!) enough to be fired. This standard is now known as Def Stan 13–131 and is the benchmark to which all munitions are measured.

Quite a lot of people have said that today's ISO 9000 originated from the 1920s munitions standard. We tend to believe, however, that the actual 'start' of ISO 9000 was probably during the US Navy Polaris submarine programme in the late 1950s when Admiral Hyman G. Rickover – for many

Figure 3.2 This is *not* a good check for Quality!

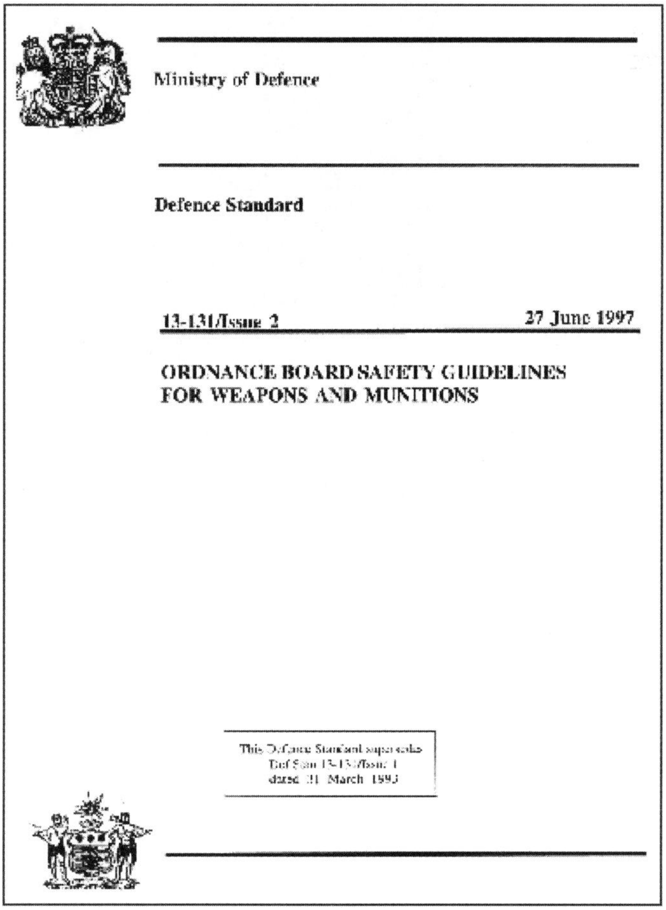

Ministry of Defence

Defence Standard

13-131/Issue 2   27 June 1997

**ORDNANCE BOARD SAFETY GUIDELINES
FOR WEAPONS AND MUNITIONS**

This Defence Standard supersedes
Def Stan 13-131/Issue 1
dated 31 March 1993

Figure 3.3 Def Stan 13–131

years the head of the US Nuclear Navy, and renowned for having a ruthless disposition and a very hot temper – became frustrated at the delays caused by defects, errors and general quality breakdowns. He took thirty fresh graduates from Harvard, gave each of them a list of subcontractors to visit and investigate, a time scale and report format and then sent them out into the industrial jungle!

When they returned and the results were analysed, Rickover discovered that there were 18 major items which were the most common, or root cause of all the problems experienced. For example:

• **wrong materials obtained** – failure to specify totally and exactly what was required on the purchase orders;

Figure 3.4 Admiral Hyman G. Rickover – The founding father of Quality?

Rickover's Results

• wrong materials obtained; etc;

• items made to wrong dimensions;

• items from different manufacturers would not fit together at the quayside;

• machines operated incorrectly – defects made in products through lack of skill;

• lack of quality control and defective items dispatched;

• status of products;

• products in doubt and no corrective actions;

• corrective actions not recognised or at best delayed, etc.

Figure 3.5 Admiral Rickover's findings

- **items made to wrong dimensions** – failure to withdraw obsolete drawings when essential design changes had been made;
- **items from different manufacturers would not fit together at the quayside** – failure to calibrate measuring instruments to reliable reference standards which differed between organisations and districts;
- **machines operated incorrectly – defects made in products through lack of skill** – failure to train operators in performing vital tasks;
- **lack of quality control and defective items dispatched** – failure to inspect effectively;
- **status of products unknown** – no records available to show what had or had not been done;
- **products in doubt and no corrective actions taken** – no appointed person to ensure operations were conducted properly;
- **corrective actions not recognised or at best delayed, etc.** – top management were unaware of what was and was not happening.

The 18 points that emerged from the survey were then used as the cornerstone for quality in the American Space Research Programme (i.e. by NASA) and eventually became the basis of the first NATO AQAP specifications which defined the quality management system requirements to be adopted by all military subcontractors.

On a similar note, NASA's first major interplanetary project – the Ranger probe, designed to impact on the surface of the Moon – nearly failed, not just because of its advanced technology and the nature of this mission, but mainly due to a total lack of project management techniques.

JPL (Jet Propulsion Laboratory), who had become the main supplier of propulsion units after NASA was founded in 1958, drew upon its previous experience as a missile arsenal and resorted initially to a 'shoot and hope' testing philosophy. After five very expensive and awful failures, NASA, justifiably fed up with all the bad publicity, called a halt to the Ranger Project and convened a project review board to try to find out what was going wrong. NASA also recommended that JPL should **not** be awarded any major new projects until the Ranger problems had been sorted out – which was quite an incentive for JPL to find out what went wrong!

One of the main points that came out of the review was that the failure reporting system mainly relied on personal contact and there was no follow-up or formal supervision. The review also concluded that the project management should be enhanced with adequate staffing, clear lines of authority, formal design reviews, and strict quality control.

With all these changes in their quality system it was hardly surprising that on July 31 1964 NASA's spacecraft was launched as planned, and sent back high resolution images, right up until the point of impact with the lunar landscape.

3.1 1979

1979 was an important year for quality standards within the United Kingdom. The British Standards Institution (BSI) had already published a number of guides on quality assurance (e.g. BS 4891:1972 – A guide to Quality Assurance). With the increased

requirements for some sort of auditable quality assurance, BSI set up a study group to produce an acceptable document that would cover all requirements for a two party manufacturing or supply contract.

This became the BS 5750 series of standards on quality systems, which were first published in the United Kingdom during 1979. These standards supplied guidelines for internal quality management as well as external quality assurance. They were quickly accepted by manufacturers, suppliers and purchasers as being a reasonable minimum level of quality assurance that they could be expected to work to. The BS 5750 series thus became the 'cornerstone' for national quality.

But in the meantime America had been working on their ANSI 90 series and other European countries were also busily developing their own sets of standards. Quite naturally, however, as the British Standards Institution had already produced and published an acceptable standard, most of these national standards were broadly based on BS 5750.

The concept was further developed by the defence, power generation, automobile and textile industries and gradually expanded from 18 initial points to 20 basic elements applicable to a very wide range of industries producing goods or services of many kinds.

3.2 1981

In 1981, the Department of Trade and Industry (DTI) formed a committee called 'FOCUS' to examine areas where standardisation could benefit the competitiveness of British manufacturers and users of high technology – for instance Local Area Network (LAN) standardisation.

Owing to the wider international interest concerning quality assurance, the International Organisation for Standardisation (ISO) then set up a Study Group during 1983 to produce an international set of standards that all countries could use.

ORGANISATION
INTERNATIONALE DE
NORMALISATION

INTERNATIONAL
ORGANIZATION FOR
STANDARDIZATION

This initiative, Open Systems Interconnection (OSI), ensured those products from different manufacturers and different countries could exchange data and interwork in certain defined areas. In the United States, the Corporation of Open Systems (COS) was formed in 1986 to pursue similar objectives.

3.3 1987

Similar to quality standards from other countries, the ISO 9000 (1987) set of standards were very heavily based on BS 5750:1979 Parts 1, 2 and 3 and followed the same sectional layout except that an additional section (ISO 9000:1987 Part 0 Section 0.1) was introduced to provide further guidance about the principal concepts and applications contained in the ISO 9000 series.

When ISO 9000 was first published in 1987 it was immediately ratified by the United Kingdom (under the direction of the Quality Management and Statistics Standards Committee) and republished by the British Standards Institution (without deviation), as the new BS 5750 (1987) standard for Quality Management Systems.

Similarly, on 10 Dec. 1987 the Technical Board of the European Committee for Standardisation Commission [Europeen de Normalisation (CEN)] approved and accepted the text of ISO 9000:1987 as the European Standard – without modification – and republished it as EN 29000:1987.

At that time official versions of EN 29000 (1987) existed in English, French and German and other CEN members were allowed to translate any of these versions into their own language; they then had the same status as the original official versions.

Note: Up-to-date lists and bibliographical references concerning these and other European standards, may be obtained on application to the CEN Central Secretariat or from any CEN member (see Useful addresses at the end of this book).

BS 5750:1987 was, therefore, identical to ISO 9000:1987 and EN 29000:1987 except that BS 5750 had three additional guidance sections. Consequently, BS 5750 was not just the British Standard for 'Quality Management Systems' it was also **the** European and **the** international standard.

But, if all of these titles referred to the same quality standard, why not call the standard by the same name?!!

3.4 1994

Well that is exactly what happened. ISO, realising the problems of calling the same document by a variety of different names was confusing (even a bit ridiculous!), reproduced (in March 1994) the ISO 9000:1994 series of documents.

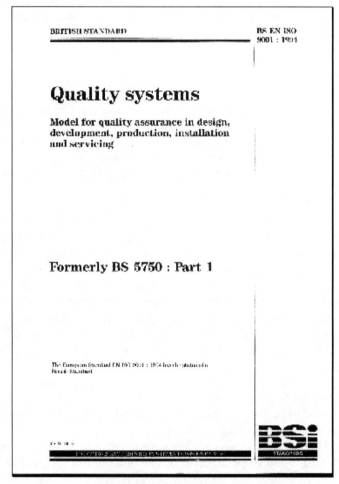

Figure 3.6 ISO 9001:1994

By the end of 1999 more than 60 countries had ratified ISO 9000 as their accepted quality standard.

Although the most notable change between the 1987 and the 1994 versions of the ISO 9000 standard was the streamlining of the numbering system, there were also around 250 other changes, the main ones being that:

- it became an explicit requirement that all members of an organisation (down to supervisory level at least) must have job profiles (descriptions) to define their authority and responsibility;
- design reviews became compulsory;
- documentation control was extended to ensure that all data was up to date.

Most of these 250 changes were intended to clarify the standard, making it easier to use. They did not significantly alter the way in which most organisations were running their businesses, merely seeking to improve it.

3.5 2000

With the end of the millennium there was no slowing down in the development of quality standards. As more and more organisations were expected to have ISO 9000 certification it became apparent that the existing structure of the standard would not suit all eventualities. This was especially relevant to the smaller organisations who did not necessarily have the resources to implement all the requirements.

With this in mind the members of ISO set about seeking the views of their members to see how the current standard could be improved. The result was the development of ISO 9001:2000.

ISO 9001:2000 is a significant refinement to ISO 9000:1994 and a more detailed explanation of its content and differences can be found in Chapter 5.

It is clear that there will be no let up in the quest for the ideal quality standard!

4 WHO PRODUCES QUALITY STANDARDS?

With literally thousands of standards available, on every conceivable topic, it can be difficult to decide which is important to you.

It has to be said, however, that standards are as international as the markets they serve and currently the main producers of national standards in Western Europe are:

- United Kingdom – British Standards Institution (BSI);
- Germany – Deutsch Institut fur Normung e.v. (DIN);
- France – Association Français de Normalisation (AFNOR).

Whilst the above countries are the primary source of European standards, there are others, as shown in Figure 4.2.

Outside Europe the most widely used standards come from:

- America – American National Standards Institute (ANSI);
- Canada – Canadian Standards Association (CSA).

There are others, of course (like Japan and Saudi Arabia), but these are the main two.

Although these countries publish what are probably the most important series of standards, virtually every country with an industrial base has its own national organisation producing its own national set of standards.

This diversity of standards can obviously lead to a lot of confusion, especially with regard to international trade and tenders. For example, if America were to invite tenders for a project quoting American (ANSI) National Standards as the minimum criteria, a European organisation could find it difficult to submit a proposal, either because it didn't have a copy of the relevant standard, or they wouldn't find it cost effective to retool their entire works in order to conform to the requirements of that particular American domestic standard.

Figure 4.1 Main producers of national standards – Europe

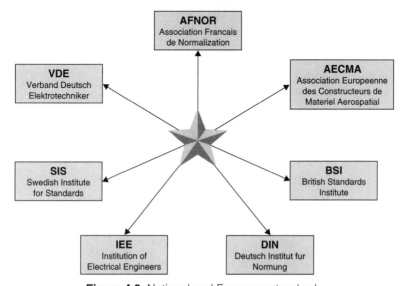

Figure 4.2 National and European standards

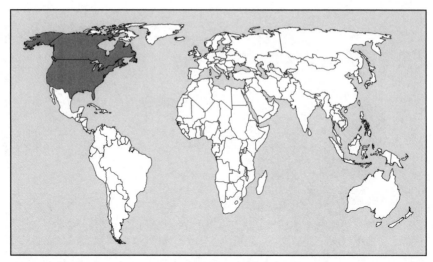

Figure 4.3 Main producers of national standards – outside Europe

In the military world the situation is little different. The United Kingdom Ministry of Defence (MOD-UK) use Defence Standards (DEF STANS), the American Division of Defense (DOD) use Military Standards (Mil-Std), the North Atlantic Treaty Organisation (NATO) use NATO Allied Quality Assurance Publications (AQAPs) and most other nations have their own particular variations.

From a more civilian point of view the International Telecommunications Union (ITU) Committees [i.e. The International Telegraph and Telephony Consultative Committee (CCITT) and the International Radio Consultative Committee (CCIR)] also publish recommendations.

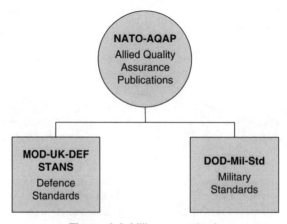

Figure 4.4 Military standards

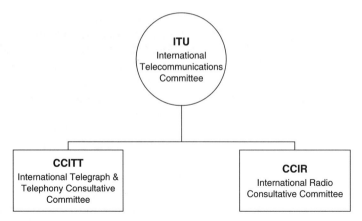

Figure 4.5 Civilian standards

Due to the diversity of publishers and publications within each country there has, therefore, been a steady growth in international standardisation and ISO and the IEC (International Electrotechnical Commission), are now the standards bodies that most countries are affiliated to – via, that is, their own particular National Standards Organisation (NSO).

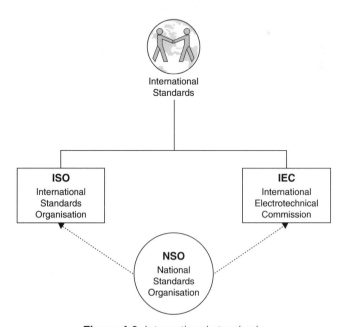

Figure 4.6 International standards

ISO which was established as a United Nations Agency in 1947 is made up of representatives from more than 90 countries and includes BSI for the United Kingdom and ANSI for the United States. The work of ISO has increased considerably since it first got underway and a great number of standards are now available and have already been adopted.

These ISO and IEC standards (ISO is mainly concerned with industrial standards whilst IEC refers to electrical equipment) were initially published as 'recommendations', but they are now accepted as international standards in their own right and the use of the word 'shall' (i.e. denoting a mandatory requirement) is becoming commonplace.

The international standards are, themselves, drawn up by International Technical Committees which have been approved by ISO or IEC member countries and there are now many hundreds of different ISO and IEC Standards available, covering virtually every situation.

However, national bodies and national standards cannot dictate customer choice. A product that may legally be marketed need not be of universal appeal or internationally acceptable (for example, the three pin electrical plug used in the UK is totally useless in other countries!). Indeed, where different national standards persist they will do so as a reflection of different market preferences and national idiosyncrasies. For industry to survive in this new, 'liberalised' market, therefore, it must have a sound technological base supported by a comprehensive set of internationally approved standards.

'Quality' has thus become the key word in today's competitive markets and there are now more than 80 countries with similar organisations – most of which are members of ISO and IEC. Figure 4.7 shows the interrelationship of these standards and committees.

From the consumer's point of view, the importance of international (i.e. ISO and IEC) standardisation is that all major agencies are now committed to recognising these standards. Equipment, modules and components can thus be designed and built so that they will be acceptable to all member countries. In this way interoperability is assured. (Perhaps, one day we may even see a European standard electrical plug!)

Thus today, there is a constant demand for new, revised and updated standards – particularly those with an international relevance. These standards could be for a product, a detailed material technical specification, broad guidelines, code of practice or for standards-based management systems. ISO 9000 (as the most successful and widely used series of Quality Management standards ever devised) have now become the benchmark for improving business efficiency and competitiveness.

It must not be forgotten, however, that the overall aim of standardisation is not just to produce paperwork that becomes part of a library. The aim is to produce a precise, succinct, readily applied and widely recognised set of principles, which are relevant and satisfy the varied needs of business, industry or commerce.

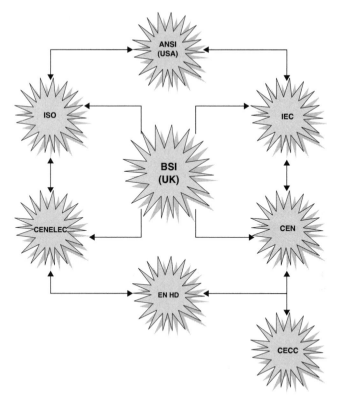

Figure 4.7 Inter-relationship of the various International Standards Bodies and Committees

The aim is also that standardisation shouldn't provide exclusive advantage to the products or services of one particular individual supplier and that the application of standards should always be capable of being verified by an independent third party evaluator (i.e. an auditor).

In the UK, the actual production of standards is set out in BS 0:1997 with its detailed:

- Guide to general principles of standardisation (Part 1);
- Guide to BSI committee procedures (Part 2);
- Guide to drafting and presentation of British Standards (Part 3).

Whilst the BSI advise that a proposal for a new standard can be made by anybody, they emphasise that the acceptance of the project by BSI has to depend on the support it can attract and, critically, the ability of the proposer – or anyone else who is able and willing – to provide an initial draft within a workable deadline. Work on new British Standards is authorised by BSI's Sector Committees. They decide the broad programme and priorities in their fields, which include consumer products and services, materials and chemicals, engineering, building and civil engineering, management systems, the electro-technical industry (for which the British Electro-Technical Committee (BEC) is responsible), healthcare and environmental concerns.

BSI committee structures correspond closely with those of other European and/or international standards organisations and their work now accounts for more than 90 per cent of the BSI standards programme. BSI also presents the British viewpoint to the European standards organisations, CEN and CENELEC, as well as ETSI in the telecommunications field. These organisations seek to develop harmonized European standards that are crucial to the success of the European Single Market. In the broader international arena, it is ISO and the IEC which pursue similar aims for harmonising world standards. Again BSI (with the BEC) is active in ensuring that the views of UK business are represented.

In all, there are more than 14,000 published ISO and IEC standards and, since the 1970s, BSI has published most of these as British Standards with a national foreword. Under European agreement, BSI also publishes European Standards (EN numbers) as identical British Standards, again with a national foreword.

5 WHAT IS ISO 9000:2000?

5.1 Background to the ISO 9001:2000 standard

When ISO 9000 was first released in 1987, it was recognised as being largely incomplete and required the auditors to fill in lots of the gaps. The first revision of ISO 9000 in 1994 got rid of many of these problems. However, an organisation could still conform to the standard but at the same time produce products that were of a consistent poor quality! There was clearly a major loophole that enabled organisations to comply with the requirements of ISO 9000:1994 but without having to **improve** their quality!

Some managers also found it extremely difficult to see the real benefit of having to commit more and more manpower and finance to maintaining their ISO 9000 certification. Whilst most organisations accepted that the

Figure 5.1 The background to ISO 9001:2000

initial certification process was worthwhile and can result in some very real benefits, these are mainly one-offs. Once ISO 9000 had been fully adopted within an organisation, it was often felt that these savings could not be repeated. The ISO 9000 certificate has been hanging on the wall in the reception office for many years but third party surveillance visits don't tell them much more than they already knew from their own internal audits.

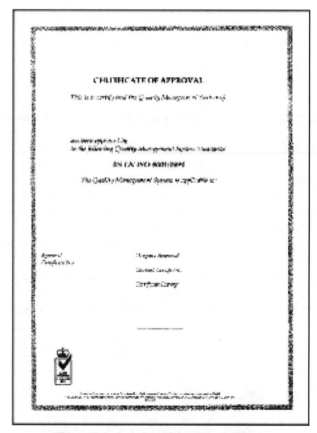

Figure 5.2 A typical ISO 9000 certificate

Quite a few organisations also felt that they had gone beyond ISO 9000 and apart from associating the organisation with a quality standard, there was little or no actual benefit to be gained from having to continually pay out for re-certification and surveillance fees.

According to the BSI, however, they frequently come across organisations who initially sought ISO 9000 certification (because it was a requirement to continue business with a client), but having seen the benefits they,

Figure 5.3 The ever-increasing demand for ISO 9000 certification

in turn, have pushed it on down their supply chain, thus increasing the requirement for ISO 9000 certification.

So as the 1990s progressed, more and more organisations started reaping benefits from the existing ISO 9000:1994 requirements but in turn also identified limitations within the series of standards. For example:

- some organisations did not need to carry out all of the 20 elements making up ISO 9001:1994 in order to be a quality organisation;
- the standard was too biased towards manufacturing industries and made it difficult for service industries to use;
- ISO 9001:1994 requirements were repeated in other management systems, resulting in duplication of effort (e.g. ISO 14001:1998 environmental management and BS8800:1996 for the management of health and safety);
- many organisations wanted to progress beyond the confines of ISO 9000 towards Total Quality Management (TQM);
- the language used was not clear and could easily be misinterpreted;
- the standard was very inflexible and could not be tailored to specific industries, etc.;
- the standard did not cater for continual improvement.

The reasons went on and on and there was clearly a need for revision.

Under existing international agreement, all International standards have to be re-inspected, 5 years after publication, for their continued applicability. In accordance with this agreement, ISO contacted more than 1,000 users and organisations for their views on ISO 9000:1994 using a questionnaire covering:

- problems with the existing standards;
- requirements for new/revised standards;
- possible harmonisation and interoperability between quality management, environmental management and health & safety standards.

The primary objective of this exercise was to make ISO 9001:2000:

- more compatible with other the management systems;
- more closely associated to business processes;
- more easily understood;
- capable of being used by all organisations, no matter their size;
- capable of used by all types of industries and professions (i.e. manufacturers **and** service providers);
- a means of continually improving quality;
- future proof.

Some of the factors considered during the development of the 2000 version of the standards included:

- problems found with ISO 9001:1994's 20 element model and its bias towards manufacturing organisations;
- the increased use of the ISO 9000 standards by regulated industries (e.g. telecommunication, aircraft and automotive industries) and the subsequent need for change;
- the proliferation of guideline standards in the current ISO 9000 family (most of which were not fully used!);
- changed user requirements with more emphasis now being on meeting customer requirements;
- the difficulties that small businesses were having in trying to meet the requirements of the standards;
- the need to be more compatible with other management system standards such as ISO 14001 for environmental management and BS8800 for occupational health and safety management;
- incorporation of the ISO 9000 standards into specific sector requirement standards or documents;
- the adoption of process-oriented management systems and the need to assist organisations in improving their business performance.

The interest shown by users in improving ISO 9000:1994 was immediately obvious by their response to the questionnaires which resulted in over 6000 comments on each of the first and second committee drafts. The results of the survey clearly showed the need for a revised ISO 9000 standard, which would:

- be split, so that one standard (i.e. ISO 9001:2000) would address requirements, whilst another (ISO 9004:2000) would address the gradual improvement of an organisation's overall quality performance;
- be simple to use, easy to understand;
- only use clear language and terminology (a definite plus for most readers of current standards!);

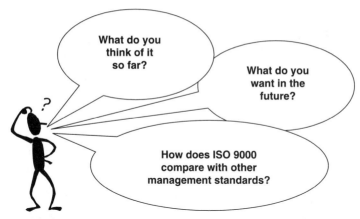

Figure 5.4 The ISO/TC 176 survey of ISO 9000:1994

- have a common structure based on a 'process model';
- be capable of being 'tailored' to fit all product and service sectors and all sizes of organisations (and not just the manufacturing industry);
- be capable of demonstrating continuous improvement and prevention of non-conformity;
- provide a natural stepping stone towards performance improvement;
- be more orientated toward continual improvement and customer satisfaction;
- have an increased compatibility with other management system standards (e.g. 14001);
- provide a basis for addressing the primary needs and interests of organisations in specific sectors such as aerospace, automotive, medical devices, telecommunications, and others.

The survey also showed that some organisations were finding it increasingly difficult to do business in the world marketplace without being ISO 9000 certified. Organisations, therefore, needed this recognition, but felt that gaining the ISO 9000 certification had been too difficult. The growing confusion about having three quality standards available for certification (i.e. ISO 9001:1994, 9002:1994 and 9003:1994) was also a problem and it was felt that the requirements of these three standards should be included into one overall standard (ISO 9001:2000).

As previously mentioned, the 2000 revision was also an attempt to harmonise the common quality management elements of ISO 9000 with those contained in the ISO 14000 series of environmental management system standards and, to some degree, the health and safety requirements of standards such as BS8800. The overall intention is to enable an organisation to run one management system that addresses quality, the environment and health and safety.

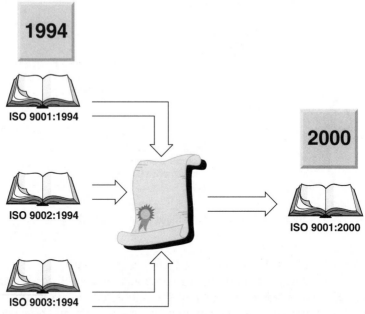

Figure 5.5 Simplified certification with only one standard

- Customer focus
- Leadership
- Involvement of people
- Process approach
- System approach
- Continual improvement
- Factual approach
- Supplier relationships

Figure 5.6 The eight quality management principles

In summary ISO 9001:2000 now:

- is flexible enough to fit any sort of organisation (i.e. the manufacturing emphasis is gone);
- no longer consists of 20 isolated elements;
- has a new quality process management model;
- defines responsibilities and authorities within the process areas;
- has a new emphasis on the identification of stakeholders and how the organisation plans to meet their needs;

- includes quality planning similar to the automotive industries advanced quality planning shown in QS 9000;
- sets a requirement for the regular review of quality objectives;
- provides a flexible approach to quality documentation;
- provides useful rules for presenting the Quality Manual;
- enables an organisation to assure that its infrastructure is sufficient to meet its quality objectives;
- provides a method for continually reviewing the work environment and its effect on quality;
- emphasises the identification and review of customer needs and expectations;
- needs a formal review of an organisation's ability to meet customer needs;
- emphasises close communications with customers;
- includes process capability studies;
- includes design control based on project management;
- includes expanded validation of design requirements;
- requires configuration management;
- gives a better definition of the function of purchasing and procurement;
- verifies purchased products;
- validates the output of processes within a organisation;
- replaces service requirements with delivery and post delivery service requirements;
- closely integrates with ISO 10012 'Measurement Management Systems' concerning the use of measurement and inspection equipment;
- needs process measurements and process audits;
- documents how a product is measured and evaluated using a Quality (Control) Plan;
- includes the requirement for regular revalidation of products or services to ensure that they continue to meet customer expectations;
- requires a formal system of measuring customer satisfaction;
- gives a more aggressive definition of corrective and preventive action;
- requires a formal policy on continuous improvement;
- is in line with other management systems/standards.

Thus all organisations, whether private or public, large or small, involved in the production of manufactured goods, services, or software, have tools available to organise their activities.

5.2 The ISO 9000:2000 family of standards

The ISO 9000:2000 family of standards consists of three primary standards. These are:

ISO 9000:2000 Quality Management Systems – Fundamentals and vocabulary (superseding ISO 8402:1994 'Quality Management and

Quality Assurance – Vocabulary' and ISO 9000–1:1994 'Quality Management and Quality Assurance Standards – Guidelines for selection and use').

Describes fundamentals of QMSs which forms the subject of the ISO 9000 family, and defines related terms.

ISO 9001:2000 Quality Management Systems – Requirements (superseding ISO 9001:1994 'Quality Systems – Model for quality assurance in design, development, production, installation and servicing', ISO 9002:1994 'Quality Systems – Model for quality assurance in production, installation and servicing' and ISO 9003:1994 'Quality Systems – Model for quality assurance in final inspection and test').

Specifies the requirements for QMSs for use where an organisation's capability to provide products that meet customer and applicable regulatory requirements needs to be demonstrated.

Figure 5.7 The ISO 9001:2000 family

ISO 9004:2000 Quality Management Systems – Guidelines for performance improvement (superseding ISO 9004–1:1994 'Quality Management and Quality System Elements – Guidelines).

Provides guidance on QMSs, including the processes for continual improvement that will contribute to the satisfaction of an organisation's customers and other interested parties.

For completeness, a new standard has been written to assist auditing systems against ISO 9001:2000, this is:

ISO 19011 Guidelines on auditing quality and environmental management systems (which supersede ISO 10011–1:1990 'Guidelines for Auditing Quality Systems – Auditing', ISO 10011–2: 1991 'Guidelines for Auditing Quality Systems – Qualification criteria for quality system auditors', ISO 10011–3:1991 'Guidelines for Auditing Quality Systems – Management of audit programmes', as well as ISO 14010:1996 'Guidelines for Environmental Auditing – General principles', ISO 14011:1996 'Guidelines for Environmental Auditing – Audit procedures – Auditing of environmental management systems' and ISO 14012:1996 'Guidelines for Environmental Auditing – Qualification criteria for environmental auditors').

This new standard provides guidance on managing and conducting environmental and quality audits.

5.2.1   ISO 9000:2000 Quality Management Systems – Fundamentals and vocabulary

Figure 5.8 The way to ISO 9000:2000

To ensure a more harmonised approach to standardisation and the achievement of coherent terminology within the ISO 9000:2000 family, the development of ISO 9000:2000 was completed in parallel with ISO 9001:2000, ISO 9004:2000, the ISO 14001 standard for environmental management and all other existing and planned management standards, most notably BS8800 for Occupational Health and Safety Management Systems.

ISO 9000:2000 provides a formal approach to the definition of terms, specifies terminology for QMSs and will assist:

- those concerned with enhancing the mutual understanding of the terminology used in quality management (e.g. suppliers, customers, regulators);
- internal or external auditors, regulators, certification and/or registration bodies;
- developers of related standards.

ISO 9000:2000 also provides an introduction to the fundamentals of Quality Management Systems.

5.2.2   ISO 9001:2000 Quality Management Systems – Requirements

Figure 5.9 The way to ISO 9001:2000

The obsolete ISO 9001:1994, ISO 9002:1994 and ISO 9003:1994 standards have now been consolidated into a single revised ISO 9001:2000 standard. Organisations that have previously used ISO 9002:1994 and ISO 9003:1994 will be allowed to be certified to ISO 9001:2000 through a *'reduction in scope'* of the standard's requirements by omitting requirements that do not apply to their particular organisation.

With the publication of ISO 9001:2000, there is now, therefore, a single quality management '**requirements**' standard that is applicable to all organisations, products and services. It is the only standard that can be used for the certification of a QMS and its generic requirements can be used by **any** organisation to:

- address customer satisfaction;
- meet customer and applicable regulatory requirements;
- enable internal and external parties (including certification bodies) to assess the organisation's ability to meet these customer and regulatory requirements.

For certification purposes, your organisation will now have to possess a documented management system which takes the inputs and transforms them into targeted outputs. Something that effectively:

- says what you are going to do;
- does what you have said you are going to do;
- keep records of everything that you do – especially when things go wrong.

The basic process to achieve these targeted outputs will encompass:

- the client's requirements;
- the inputs from management and staff;
- documented controls for any activities that are needed to produce the finished article;
- record keeping to prove product compliance to customer requirements;
- and, of course, delivering a product or service which satisfies the customer's original requirements.

Figure 5.10 The basic process

The adoption of a QMS has to be a strategic decision of any organisation and the design and implementation of their QMS will be influenced by its varying needs, objectives, products provided, processes employed and the size and structure of that organisation. As ISO are quick to point out, however, it is not the intention of ISO 9001:2000 to insist on a uniform structure to QMSs, or uniformity of documentation and the QMS requirements specified in this standard should always be viewed as complementary to product technical requirements.

The ISO 9001:2000 standard is the only standard within the 2000 edition to which an organisation can be certified. It includes all the key points from the previous 20 elements of ISO 9001:1994, but integrates them into four major generic business processes, namely:

- **Management responsibility** (policy, objectives, planning, system, review);
- **Resource management** (human resources, information, facilities);
- **Product realisation** (customer, design, purchasing, production, calibration);
- **Measurement, analysis and improvement** (audit, process/product control, improvement).

Figure 5.11 The four major generic business processes of ISO 9001:2000

The new structure of ISO 9001:2000 is as shown in Table 5.1.

5.3 The 'consistent pair'

In providing the new standards, ISO developed ISO 9001:2000 and ISO 9004:2000 with the same sequence and structure; so that it could form a 'consistent pair' of quality management standards which can be used either together or independently.

Whilst ISO 9001:2000 specifies the requirements for a QMS (that can be used by organisations for certification or contractual purposes),

Table 5.1 The structure of ISO 9001:2000

Section	Title
1	**Scope**
1.1	General
1.2	Application
2	**Normative reference**
3	**Terms and definitions**
4	**Quality Management System**
4.1	General requirements
4.2	Documentation requirements
4.2.1	General
4.2.2	Quality Manual
4.2.3	Control of documents
4.2.4	Control of quality records
5	**Management responsibility**
5.1	Management commitment
5.2	Customer focus
5.3	Quality policy
5.4	Planning
5.4.1	Quality objectives
5.4.2	Quality management system planning
5.5	Responsibility, authority and communication
5.5.1	Responsibility and authority
5.5.2	Management representative
5.5.3	Internal communication
5.6	Management review
5.6.1	General
5.6.2	Review input
5.6.3	Review output
6	**Resource management**
6.1	Provision of resources
6.2	Human resources
6.2.1	General
6.2.2	Competence, awareness and training
6.3	Infrastructure
6.4	Work environment
7	**Product realisation**
7.1	Planning of product realisation
7.2	Customer-related processes
7.2.1	Determination of requirements related to the product
7.2.2	Review of requirements related to the product

Table 5.1 *Continued*

Section	Title
7.2.3	Customer communication
7.3	Design and development
7.3.1	Design and development planning
7.3.2	Design and development inputs
7.3.3	Design and development outputs
7.3.4	Design and development review
7.3.5	Design and development verification
7.3.6	Design and development validation
7.3.7	Control of design and development changes
7.4	Purchasing
7.4.1	Purchasing process
7.4.2	Purchasing information
7.4.3	Verification of purchased product
7.5	Production and service provision
7.5.1	Control of production and service provision
7.5.2	Validation of processes for production and service provision
7.5.3	Identification and traceability
7.5.4	Customer property
7.5.5	Preservation of product
7.6	Control of measuring and monitoring devices
8	**Measurement, analysis and improvement**
8.1	General
8.2	Monitoring and measurement
8.2.1	Customer satisfaction
8.2.2	Internal audit
8.2.3	Monitoring and measurement of processes
8.2.4	Monitoring and measurement of product
8.3	Control of non-conformity
8.4	Analysis of data
8.5	Improvement
8.5.1	Continual improvement
8.5.2	Corrective action
8.5.3	Preventive action

Note – A basic explanation of each of these clauses can be found in Annex A at the rear of this book.

ISO 9004:2000 provides guidance aimed at improving an organisation's overall quality performance. ISO 9004:2000 is not, however, meant as a 'guideline for implementing ISO 9001:2000' nor is it intended for certification or contractual use.

Both of the standards are based on eight quality management principles, which reflect best management practices. These eight principles are:

- customer focus;
- leadership;
- involvement of people;
- process approach;
- system approach to management;
- continual improvement;
- factual approach to decision making;
- mutually beneficial supplier relationship.

These principles are expanded upon in Section 5.5.

5.4 Compatibility with other Management Systems

Most businesses strive to achieve three major goals:

1 Producing consistently acceptable products/services that satisfy their customers and, hence result in repeat orders and thereby increase profit levels.
   i.e. **QUALITY**
2 Striving to prevent any unnecessary damage to the natural world when carrying out their business.
   i.e. **ENVIRONMENT**
3 Avoiding injuring their staff and ensuring their welfare.
   i.e. **SAFETY**

Standards for management systems covering these three fundamentals to business success are covered within ISO 9001, ISO 14001 and BS8800 respectively.

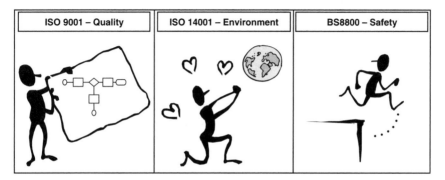

| ISO 9001 – Quality | ISO 14001 – Environment | BS8800 – Safety |

Figure 5.12

All three of these standards have been written with a degree of commonality, with the specific aim of enabling businesses to produce single unified management systems that embrace Quality, Environment and Safety. This type of system is generally referred to as an Integrated Management System. Obviously it makes great commercial sense to have one business management system covering all three, as it avoids duplication.

ISO 9001:2000 does not, however, make any specific reference to any other management system standard, it does nevertheless, allow an organisation to align and integrate its own QMS with other related management system requirements. In essence by taking ISO 9001:2000 as the foundation of an integrated management system, it is possible to 'bolt on' the additional requirements of other management system standards.

Figure 5.13 The Common Elements of ISO 9001, 14001 and BS8800

As more management system standards are developed you can expect to see many showing a similar degree of commonality.

5.4.1   Compatibility with ISO 14001:1996

In producing ISO 9001:2000, the drafting committee (TC176) made sure that the requirements of ISO 14001:1996 'Environmental management systems – Specification with guidance for use' have been considered and a very good degree of compatibility now exists between the two standards. Work is now underway to revise ISO 14001 to bring it even further in line.

5.4.2 Compatibility with BS8800:2004

This British Standard, providing guidance on Occupational Health and Safety (OHS) management systems, whilst not yet having International (i.e. ISO) status is generally accepted as defining the minimum requirements needed to control OHS risks, improve its performance and assists in complying with safety legislation.

As with ISO 9001 and 14001 it follows the common strands of good business management.

Prior to the release of BS8800:2004, the internationally recognised assessment specification OHSAS 18001:1999 was developed. It was produced in response to urgent demands for a recognisable model against which management systems could be evaluated and also for guidance on how to set up a OHS management system.

The OHSAS 18001 specification does not have the status of a British or International Standard. As such, BS8800 is used to deliver OHSAS 18001 compliant occupational health and safety management systems.

5.5 The Principles of ISO 9001:2000

5.5.1 Eight Principles of Management

ISO 9001:2000 is the internationally recognised standard for quality management systems. As such, it provides the benchmark against which a company's management system is measured and, if found to be adequate, certified as compliant. Consequently, for this standard to be seen as the leading example of management system methodology it had to reflect currently accepted best practice.

With this in mind the standard was developed to be totally business focused, aimed at improving an organisation's management system through the application of eight proven principles:

Customer Focus

Seeking to satisfy the demands and expectations of the purchaser.

Organisations depend on their customers and should, therefore:

- understand current and future customer needs;
- meet customer requirements;
- strive to exceed customer expectations.

Figure 5.14 *The Eight Principles*

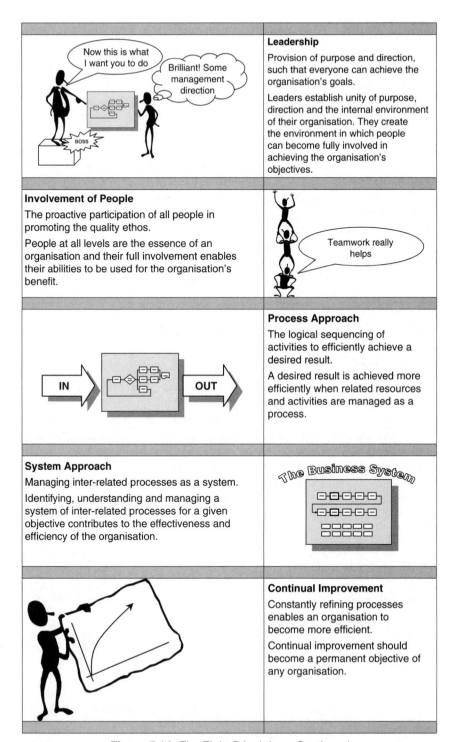

Figure 5.14 *The Eight Principles – Continued*

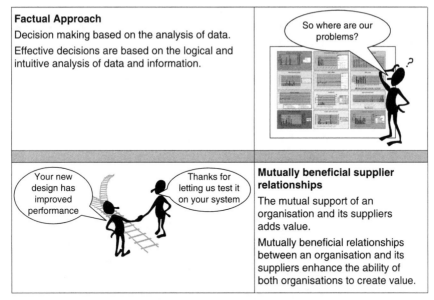

Figure 5.14 *The Eight Principles – Continued*

5.5.2   The Process Model

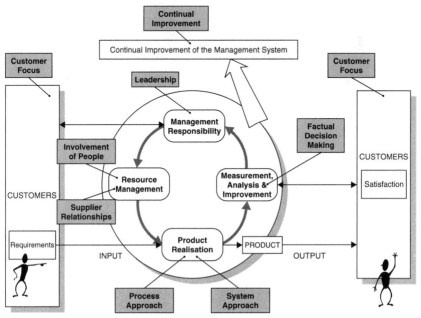

Figure 5.15 The ISO 9001:2000 Process Model and the eight management principles

The eight management principles are reflected in the ISO 9001 process model shown on p. 117, indicating how each of these principles is embraced within the ethos of the standard.

Throughout ISO 9001:2000, the requirement for continuous improvement is frequently (and heavily) emphasised. The process model in Figure 5.12 clearly shows how the four major sections of ISO 9001:2000 interrelate (i.e. management responsibility, resource management, product realisation, measurement, analysis and improvement) and how the improvement processes continuously revolve around all other aspects of quality management.

Each of these four sections is then sub-divided into a series of elements or sub-sections but, the most important element is Section 5.1 (Management

Figure 5.16 ISO 9001:2000 for Small Businesses

commitment) which states that *'top management shall provide evidence of its commitment to the development and implementation of the Quality Management System and continually improving its effectiveness'*.

5.6 Brief summary of ISO 9001:2000 requirements

ISO 9001:2000 consists of eight sections which are summarised below. For a more complete description please see *ISO 9001:2000 for Small Businesses,* 3rd edn, by Ray Tricker from Butterworth-Heinemann's 'ISO 9000:2000' series.

5.6.1   Section 1 – Scope

This is a short section explaining what the standard covers.

5.6.2   Section 2 – Normative reference

Another short section which contains details of other standards that form a mandatory input to ISO 9001:2000. In this instance the only reference is ISO 9000:2000 'Quality Management Systems – Fundamentals and vocabulary'.

5.6.3   Section 3 – Terms and definitions

The third section explains how the standard is based on a supply chain concept as shown in Figure 5.17.

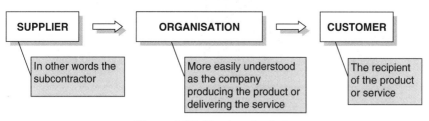

Figure 5.17 The supply chain

5.6.4   Section 4 – Quality Management System

This section makes it mandatory for an organisation to have a documented QMS that defines the processes necessary to ensure that the product conforms to customer requirements. This QMS must be implemented, maintained and, most importantly, continually improved by the organisation.

It should be noted that the extent of the QMS documentation (which may be in any form or type of medium) is dependent on the:

- size and type of the organisation;
- complexity and interaction of the processes;
- competency of personnel.

5.6.5   Section 5 – Management responsibility

This section is broken down into the following sub-clauses that cover the requirements for:

- **Management commitment** – top (i.e. senior) management committing, fully, to the development and implementation of the QMS and continually improving its effectiveness. (Without their commitment the system will fall at the first hurdle);

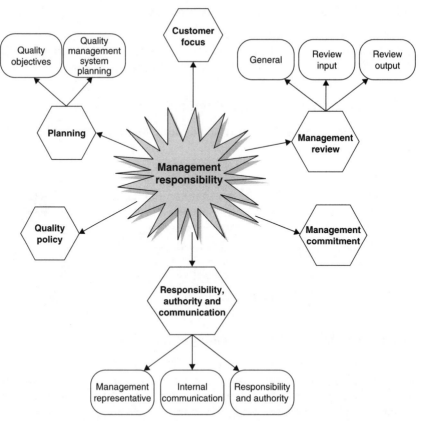

Figure 5.18 Section 5 – Management responsibility

- **Customer focus** – determining, fully understanding and documenting customer requirements; ensuring compliance with identified statutory legislation (e.g. EC Directives, other national and international standards etc.);
- **Quality policy** – ensuring that the Quality Policy is appropriate for the purpose, includes a commitment to comply with requirements (and improve the effectiveness of the QMS), is understood by everyone and reviewed for continued suitability;
- **Planning** – clearly stating management's quality objectives and policy with regards to quality in an established, fully documented, QMS;
- **Responsibility, Authority and Communication** – ensuring that the responsibilities, authorities and their interrelations are defined (and communicated) within the organisation;
- **Management representative** – appointing someone (or some people) to be responsible for the implementation and improvement of the organisation's QMS;
- **Management review** – carrying out regular reviews of the QMS to ensure it continues to function correctly (and to identify areas for improvement).

5.6.6   Section 6 – Resource management

This section covers resources with regard to training, induction, responsibilities, working environment, equipment requirements, maintenance etc.

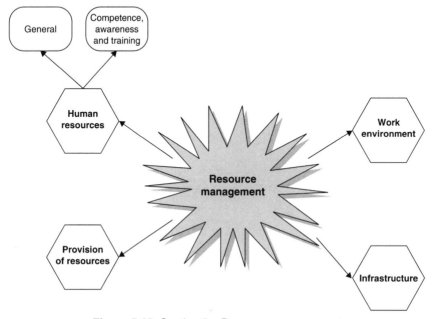

Figure 5.19 Section 6 – Resource management

It is broken down into the following sub-sections that cover the require-ments for:

- **Provision of resources** – identifying the resources required to imple-ment and improve the processes that make up the QMS;
- **Human resources** – assigning personnel with regard to competency, education, training, skill and/or experience;
- **Facilities** – identifying, providing and maintaining the workspace, facil-ities, equipment (hardware and software) and supporting services to achieve conformity of product;
- **Work environment** – identifying and managing the work environment (e.g. health and safety, ambient conditions etc.).

5.6.7   Section 7 – Product realisation

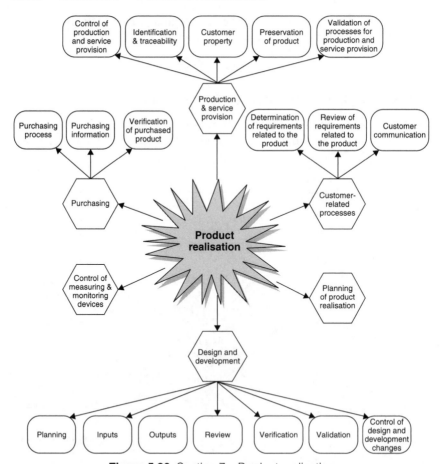

Figure 5.20 Section 7 – Product realisation

This section is fundamentally concerned with how a product or service is planned and turned to reality, and is broken down into a number of sub-sections that cover the requirements for:

- **Planning product realisation** – clearly defining and documenting the processes used to ensure reliable and consistent products (e.g. verification and validation activities, criteria for acceptability and quality records etc.);
- **Customer-related processes** – identifying customer, product, legal and design requirements;
- **Design and development** – controlling the design process (e.g. design inputs, outputs, review, verification, validation and change control);
- **Purchasing** – having documented processes for the selection and control of suppliers and the control of purchases that affect the quality of the finished product or service;
- **Production and service provision** – having documented instructions that control the manufacture of a product or delivery of a service;
- **Control of measuring and monitoring devices** – their control, calibration and protection.

5.6.8   Section 8 – Measurement, analysis and improvement

This section covers the tools needed to ensure product compliance and those required to improve the QMS. It includes requirements for:

- **Planning** – defining the requirements for measurement analysis and improvement (including statistical analysis);
- **Customer satisfaction** – monitoring customer satisfaction/dissatisfaction as a measurement and improvement of the QMS;
- **Internal audits** – conducting periodic internal audits to confirm continued conformity with ISO 9001:2000;
- **Measurement and monitoring of processes and product** – defining processes to monitor the performance of the QMS and the products and services delivered by the organisation;
- **Non-conformity** – controlling non-conformity and its rectification;
- **Data analysis** – collecting and analysing statistical data obtained from the organisation's measuring and monitoring activities to find areas of improvement;
- **Improvement** – planning for continual improvement of the QMS;
- **Corrective and preventive action** – having available procedures to address corrective and preventive action.

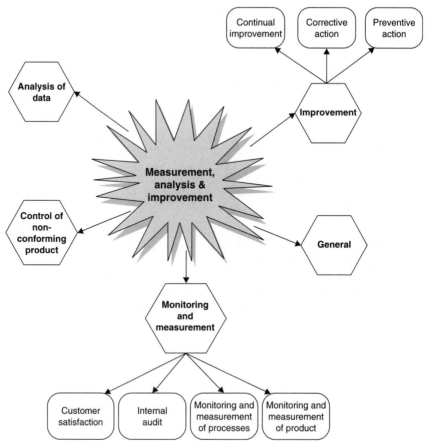

Figure 5.21 Section 8 – Measurement, analysis and improvement

5.7 ISO 9004:2000 Quality Management Systems – guidelines for performance improvement

ISO 9004:2000 provides guidance on QMSs, including the processes that are required for continual improvement and, ultimately, customer satisfaction. The guidance should be viewed as generic and with the overall aim of being applicable to all organisations, regardless of the type, size and the product provided. It is based on the provisions of the ISO 9004:1994 series.

ISO 9004:2000 is aimed at improving an organisation's overall quality performance and provides a stepping stone to Total Quality Management (TQM). In the words of the standard, *'ISO 9004:2000 is designed to go beyond quality management requirements and provide organisations with*

Figure 5.22 The reason for ISO 9004:2000

guidelines for performance improvement through sustained customer sat-isfaction. In doing so it:

- *provides guidance to management on the application and use of a QMS to improve an organisation's overall performance;*
- *is recommended as a guide for organisations whose management wishes to move beyond the minimum requirements of ISO 9001 in pursuit of increased performance improvement ISO 9004 is not intended as guidance for compliance with ISO 9001;*
- *defines the minimum QMS requirements needed to achieve customer satisfaction by meeting specified product requirements;*
- *can be also be used by an organisation to demonstrate its capability to meet customer requirements'.*

Note: This international standard is not a guideline for implementing ISO 9001 and is not intended for certification, regulatory or contractual use.

6 HOW QUALITY HELPS DURING A PRODUCT'S LIFE CYCLE

In the previous chapters we learnt how to produce a correctly structured Quality Management System (QMS) and in Chapter 5 we saw the requirements that this QMS would have to meet. However, you may well still be saying, that is all well and good, but how will it help me improve quality in my organisation?

In this chapter we will look at all the areas that can be influenced by quality during the life of a product. This will clearly show even the most cynical of readers that there is no part of a business that cannot be improved by incorporating quality into your management system.

To start with you have to appreciate that there are a number of stages during a product's lifecycle where quality assurance has an influence.

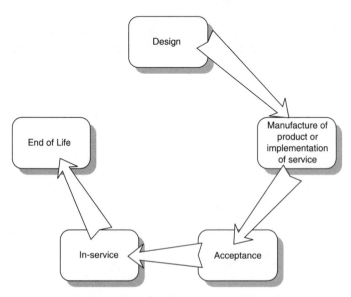

Figure 6.1 Quality Assurance lifecycle

6.1 Design stage

'Quality must be designed into a product before manufacture or assembly'
(ISO 9004:2000).

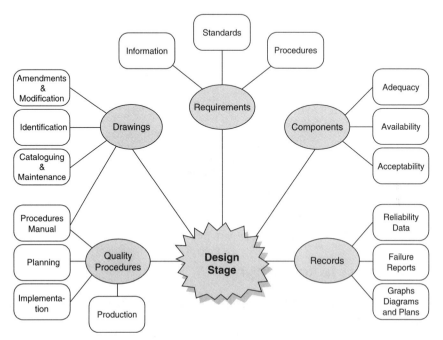

Figure 6.2 Design stage

Throughout the design stage of a product the quality of that design must be regularly checked. Quality Processes and Procedures (QPs) have to be planned, written and implemented so as to predict and evaluate the fundamental and intrinsic reliability of the proposed design.

It is at this time that the proposed design is verified against the customer requirements to ensure it will actually deliver the intended functionality.

6.2 Manufacturing stage

'Manufacturing operations must be carried out under controlled conditions' (ISO 9004:2000).

During all manufacturing processes, (and throughout early in-service life), the product must be subjected to a variety of quality control procedures and checks in order to evaluate the degree of quality. These controls will ensure the product complies with your predetermined documented requirements.

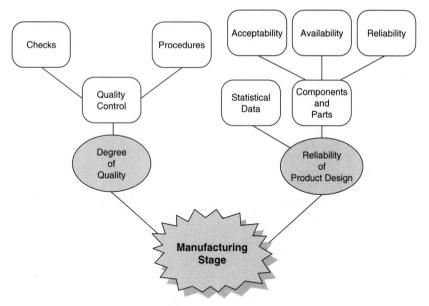

Figure 6.3 Manufacturing stage

6.3 Acceptance stage

'The Quality of a product must be proved before being accepted' (ISO 9004:2000).

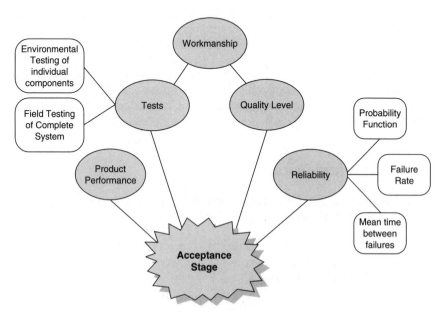

Figure 6.4 Acceptance stage

During the acceptance stage, the product is subjected to a series of tests designed to confirm that the workmanship of the product fully meets the levels of quality required (or stipulated) by the user and that the product performs the required function correctly. Tests will range from environmental tests of individual components to field testing complete products.

This acceptance stage is generally termed the 'Validation' phase, where a finished product is checked to ensure it complies with the original requirements.

6.4 In-service stage

'Evaluation of product performance during typical operating conditions and feedback of information gained through field use – improves product capability' (ISO 9004:2000).

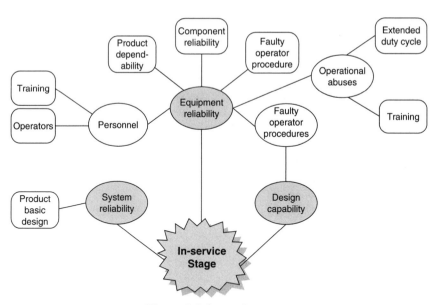

Figure 6.5 In-service stage

During the in-service stage the equipment user is, of course, principally concerned with product reliability.

Customer feedback is an important part of the In-service stage as it will assist in improving the product or service for future versions.

6.5 End of life stage

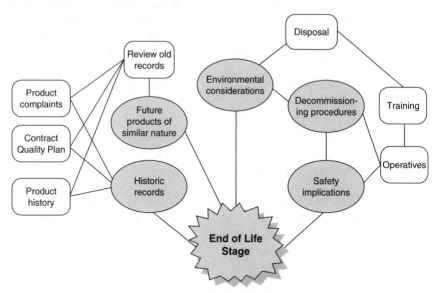

Figure 6.6 End of life stage

Designing, manufacturing, accepting and using a product is not the full story. Eventually that product will come to the end of its useful life either through age, fault or more than likely (because it has been built to such a high quality!) it has been overtaken by technology. Before throwing the redundant piece of equipment onto the rubbish heap, however, it is essential that a fully documented, historical record, of its design, use, problems, advantages and disadvantages etc. is assembled. This would normally be left up to the Quality Manager to organise.

So if you can incorporate quality into all five stages within the life of a product then you can have total control over your own success ... or failure!

WHO CONTROLS QUALITY IN AN ORGANISATION?

Do not think for one minute that quality is the sole responsibility of the Quality Manager. You would even be wrong to think that the buck stops with senior management. Why not the staff? After all, they are responsible for physically incorporating quality into a product. Some may even foolishly say that the Quality Manual sitting on the shelf is the only control they need. The answer to who controls quality is very simple. **Everyone and everything** within an organisation has a part to play.

So what responsibilities do each of these groups of people have?

Who Controls Quality in a company?

The Quality Management Team?   Management?   The staff?

Figure 7.1 Everyone has an impact on quality

7.1 Management

The main requirement of the organisation's management is that they establish, define and document their organisation's policy, objectives and commitments to quality.

As we have seen in the previous chapters, this documented system is usually presented as a Quality Manual. The Quality Manual must include details of the organisation's QMS and the aims, policies, organisation and procedures that are essential to demonstrate that they agree with the requirements of the relevant standard (e.g. ISO 9000 or ISO 14000).

Having established their overall position, the management will then have to:

- develop, control, co-ordinate, supervise and monitor their corporate quality policy and ensure that this policy is understood and maintained throughout the organisation;
- ensure that the organisation's QMS always meets the requirements of the national, European or international standard that the particular organisation has chosen to work to and where this fails to happen, see that corrective actions are carried out;
- define objectives such as fitness for use;
- ensure that the performance, safety and reliability of a product is correct and make sure that the costs associated with these objectives are kept to a reasonable figure.

7.1.1 The 21 Management responsibilities

The standard demands approximately 270 separate requirements of management, but none are as important as the 21 responsibilities expected specifically of senior management, by which they mean the Managing Director and functional heads.

To avoid any confusion or any element of doubt over what is expected of senior management (the standard refers to them as Top Management), ISO 9001:2000 very clearly defines their responsibilities. They are as follows:

Top Management shall:		
1.	provide evidence of its commitment to the development and implementation of the Quality Management System and continually improving its effectiveness by:	Clause 5.1
2.	a) communicating to the organisation the importance of meeting customer as well as statutory and regulatory requirements,	(see also 5.2)

3.	b) establishing the quality policy,	(see also 5.3)
4.	c) ensuring that quality objectives are established,	(see also 5.4.1)
5.	d) conducting management reviews,	(see also 5.6.1)
6.	e) ensuring the availability of resources.	
7.	ensure that customer requirements are determined and are met with the aim of enhancing customer satisfaction.	Clause 5.2
8.	ensure that the quality policy: a) is appropriate to the purpose of the organisation,	Clause 5.3
9.	b) includes a commitment to comply with requirements and continually improve the effectiveness of the quality management system,	Clause 5.3
10.	c) provides a framework for establishing and reviewing quality objectives,	Clause 5.3
11.	d) is communicated and understood within the organisation,	Clause 5.3
12.	e) is reviewed for continuing suitability.	
13.	ensure that quality objectives, including those needed to meet requirements for product, are established at relevant functions and levels within the organisation. (The quality objectives shall be measurable, and consistent with the quality policy.)	Clause 5.4.1
14.	ensure that the planning of the quality management system is carried out in order to meet the requirements given in 4.1 (Quality Management System – General requirements), as well as the quality objectives.	Clause 5.4.2.a
15.	ensure that the integrity of the Quality Management System is maintained when changes to the Quality Management System are planned and implemented.	Clause 5.4.2.b

(Continued)

16.	ensure that responsibilities and authorities are defined and communicated within the organisation.	Clause 5.5.1
17.	appoint a member of management who, irrespective of other responsibilities, shall have responsibility and authority that includes: a) ensuring that processes needed for the Quality Management System are established, implemented and maintained, b) reporting to top management on the perform- ance of the Quality Management System and any need for improvement, c) ensuring the promotion of awareness of customer requirements throughout the organisation. (Note: The responsibility of a management repre- sentative can include liaison with external parties on matters relating to the quality management system.)	Clause 5.5.2
18.	ensure that appropriate communication processes are established within the organisation, ...	Clause 5.5.3
19.	and that communication takes place regarding the effectiveness of the Quality Management System.	
20.	review the organisation's Quality Management System, at planned intervals, to ensure its continuing suitability, adequacy and effectiveness.	Clause 5.6.1
21.	This review shall include assessing opportunities for improvement and the need for changes to the Quality Management System, including the Quality Policy and Quality Objectives.	

Of those responsibilities listed above none is more important than the first. Without senior management committing to the development and imple- mentation of the QMS your venture into the world of process based busi- ness management is doomed from the start. Put another way, your customers may demand quality, your staff may be prepared to deliver it but if the boss is not fussed then at very least expect your business to stag- nate, or at worst go bust through lack of commitment.

A business management system is only as successful as the commit- ment put in from the top.

In conclusion, senior management responsibilities include:

- committing to the implementation and development of a Quality Management System;

- ensuring that customer requirements are recognised, endorsed and met;
- developing a Quality Policy, supported by measurable Quality Objectives;
- planning the Quality Management System and ensuring its continued integrity;
- setting and communicating responsibilities and authorities;
- assigning a management representative as the Quality Manager;
- establishing and using internal communication processes;
- reviewing the Quality Management System at planned intervals.

7.2 Quality management team

As previously described, quality assurance is concerned with a consistency of quality and an agreed level of quality. To achieve these aims an organisation must be firmly committed to the fundamental principle of consistently supplying the right quality product. Equally, a purchaser must be committed to the fundamental principle of only accepting the right quality product.

Thus, a commitment within all levels of an organisation to the basic principles of quality assurance and quality control is required. It is, therefore, essential that a completely separate and independent division is formed to deal solely with quality matters. The organisation and duties of this section would usually look something like that shown in Figure 7.2.

It is important to note that the Quality Manager answers directly to the Managing Director and not through one of the MD's line managers. It is only in this way that the Quality Manager can be truly independent and be allowed to report all issues (good and bad) to the MD without fear of retribution!

A Managing Director must have complete trust in his Quality Manager and, conversely, the Quality Manager must be allowed to pass on the news of process failings without recourse to any of those people responsible for carrying them out.

Do not, however, think that a Quality Manager is a quisling prepared to name and shame managers or their staff when they fail to perform a process correctly. It is rarely the fault of people that things go wrong; it is generally the fault of the process or a lack of training. As such the Quality Manager should be looking for ways of rectifying the process or recommending ways of filling knowledge gaps.

For organisations who cannot justify the cost of employing full time quality departments, other options are available, such as:

- selecting personnel from existing staff who are not directly involved with a production process. They are then able to act as independent unbiased assessors;
- employing third party quality consultants, on a temporary basis, to carry out fully independent quality inspections and audits.

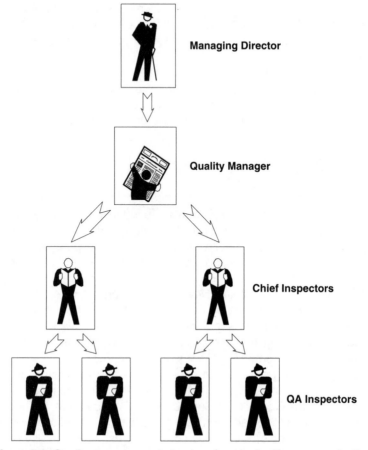

Managing Director

Quality Manager

Chief Inspectors

QA Inspectors

Figure 7.2 Quality management structure for a typical large organisation

7.2.1 Quality Manager

The first requirement is for the organisation to nominate an individual who will be solely responsible to the management for the implementation and maintenance of the Quality Management System. This person is generally called the 'Quality Manager', although in some enlightened companies they are referred to as Business Systems Managers.

The Quality Manager will answer directly to the Managing Director and will be responsible for all matters regarding the quality of the end product together with the activities of **all** sections within the organisation's premises.

Whilst there is a specific requirement within ISO 9001:2000 to appoint a member of staff to be directly responsible for quality management, this doesn't mean that you necessarily **have** to have a Quality Manager. In small organisations quality management might be part of the General Manager's duties. Regardless of who it may be, however, it is essential that this person is someone who is completely independent of any manufacturing or user function and has a thorough working knowledge of the requirements and recommendations of ISO 9001:2000.

In addition, owing to the importance of quality assurance, it is essential that the person selected for this position is fully qualified (both technically and administratively) and can quickly exert (show) his position and authority.

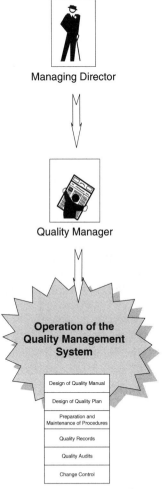

Managing Director

Quality Manager

Operation of the Quality Management System

Design of Quality Manual

Design of Quality Plan

Preparation and Maintenance of Procedures

Quality Records

Quality Audits

Change Control

Figure 7.3 Responsibilities of the Quality Manager

The Quality Manager's job is usually a very busy one, even in a small organisation(!) and the Quality Manager's responsibilities are spread over a wide area which covers all of the organisation's operations, as shown below.

7.2.1.1 General functional description

The Quality Manager is responsible for ensuring that the organisation's QMS is defined, implemented, audited and monitored in order to ensure that the organisation's deliverables comply with both the customer's requirements together with the requirements of ISO 9001:2000.

7.2.1.2 Tasks

The Quality Manager normally reports directly to the Managing Director. His tasks shall include:

- ensuring the consistency of the organisation's QMS;
- ensuring compliance of the organisation's QMS with ISO 9001:2000;
- maintenance and effectiveness of the organisation's QMS;
- ensuring that the quality message is transmitted to and understood by everyone.

7.2.1.3 Responsibilities

The Quality Manager is responsible for:

- ensuring that the Quality Manual and individual Quality Plans are kept up to date;
- assisting and advising with the preparation of organisation's procedures;
- producing, reviewing and updating the organisation's QMS;
- ensuring compliance with the organisation's QMS by means of frequent audits;
- maintaining organisation quality records;
- producing, auditing and maintaining project Quality Plans;
- identifying potential/current problem areas within the organisation's life cycle through analysis of organisation statistics;
- holding regular quality audits.

7.2.1.4 Co-ordination

The Quality Manager shall:

- act as the focal point for all organisation quality matters within the organisation;
- co-ordinate and verify that all internal procedures and instructions are in accordance with the requirements of ISO 9001:2000 and the recommendations of ISO 9004:2000;
- operate the QMS as described in the Quality Manual and ensure that its regulations are observed.

Above all the Quality Manager must always ensure that the customer's interests are protected. Even if this means, at times, that he becomes very unpopular with the rest of the organisation and sometimes they even have to assume the mantel of organisation 'scapegoat'!

7.2.2 Chief Quality Assurance Inspector

Depending upon its size and activities, there may be more than one chief Quality Assurance Inspector (QAI) in an organisation.

The duties of the Chief QAI are to:

- plan, co-ordinate and supervise all pre-shop, in-process, and out-going inspections within their area of responsibility;

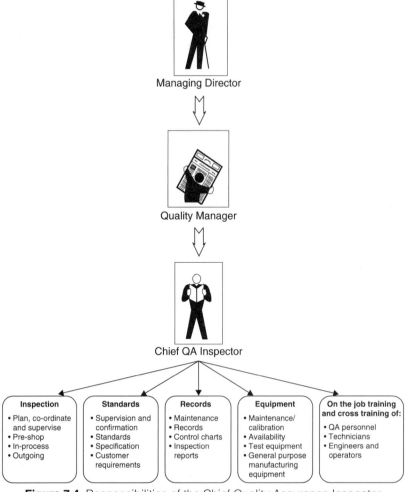

Managing Director

Quality Manager

Chief QA Inspector

Inspection	Standards	Records	Equipment	On the job training and cross training of:
• Plan, co-ordinate and supervise • Pre-shop • In-process • Outgoing	• Supervision and confirmation • Standards • Specification • Customer requirements	• Maintenance • Records • Control charts • Inspection reports	• Maintenance/ calibration • Availability • Test equipment • General purpose manufacturing equipment	• QA personnel • Technicians • Engineers and operators

Figure 7.4 Responsibilities of the Chief Quality Assurance Inspector

- ensure that the product is in agreement with the customers' requirements and conform to the established quality standards and specifications;
- be responsible for scheduling and controlling inspections, designating inspection stations, setting up local inspection procedures and statistical inspection controls;
- oversee the maintenance of inspection records, control charts and the preparation of inspection reports;
- ensure that all test equipment is maintained, properly calibrated and readily available at all inspection stations;
- be responsible for reviewing the maintenance of quality inspection stations;
- co-ordinate on-the-job and cross training within sections;
- establish and maintain inspection systems and controls to determine the acceptability of a completed product;
- be responsible for detecting deficiencies during manufacture, initiate corrective actions where applicable and prevent defects;
- compile quality and feedback data, quality history and statistical results to help quality control development, refinement and management;
- advise management and key maintenance personnel on all aspects concerning quality trends.

Within smaller organisations the role of Chief QAI is most likely to be taken on as part of the duties of a senior member of shop floor staff.

7.2.3 Section Quality Assurance Inspectors

Two Section QAIs are normally nominated for each area, a principal and an alternate. The principal is always the Assurer, the alternate assumes

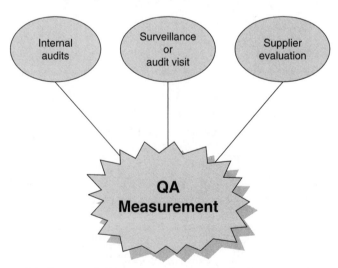

Figure 7.5 Responsibilities of the Section Quality Assurance Inspector

the duties when asked to do so by the principal and during the absence of the principal. When not engaged on QA duties, the QAIs are employed on normal workshop activities.

The task of the section QAI is to:

- review (and make recommendations) to the chief QAI on all things concerning engineering change proposals, waivers, deviations and substitution of parts, materials, equipment and processes;
- compile quality feedback data and quality history sheets;
- supply technical data and assistance to the design office.

7.2.4 Quality Assurance personnel

Quality Assurance (QA) personnel are members of an organisation judged competent to carry out quality assurance duties. They are nominated by the Quality Manager in consultation with the QAIs and are directly responsible to the Quality Manager when engaged in QA work.

QA personnel are:

- not to allow their own judgement to be influenced by others;
- not to allow products (or services) to leave the premises below the desired standard;
- to ensure – by close liaison with section chiefs - that a section's work is not unreasonably delayed because of QA;
- to ensure that when a 'job' (i.e. service, system, module or equipment etc.) fails their inspection that the respective Section QAI is informed and that the section chief (and technician responsible) are made fully aware of the reasons for the failure;
- to advise the section quality assurance inspector of any problems associated with quality assurance, particularly anything that is likely to effect production or harmony between any of the sections and the quality assurance division.

7.2.5 The staff

Your staff are at the sharp end of delivering quality. They are responsible for implementing the quality control processes that will ensure the desired level of quality is consistently applied to the product. Of course they are not responsible for setting the level of quality but, so long as they have been clearly briefed on what is required and have received the appropriate training to do the job, they will be capable of delivering that level of quality.

It is vital that a workforce is as committed to quality as the management. A committed workforce will look after your organisation. A workforce who is empowered to implement quality (and are allowed to have an input into defining and improving it) will be highly motivated. Morale will improve as staff will feel that they are doing a good job that they can be proud of.

In summary, an organisation's workforce has the responsibility for:

- working in accordance with the predefined WIs;
- refusing to accept anything that is substandard;
- having an active role in quality improvements;
- having an input into defining levels of quality (after all, they know better than anybody what can be achieved);
- delivering the level of quality specified in the QMS.

In short, your staff are your greatest asset.

Figure 7.6 Recognise your greatest asset!

7.3 Quality Assurance resources

It is not enough for management to supply just the personnel for a QA section. Resources, appropriate for the implementation of the quality policies, must also be available.

These shall include:

- management budget;
- training budget;
- design and development equipment;
- manufacturing equipment;
- inspection, test and examination equipment;
- instrumentation and computer software.

8 WHAT ARE THE PURCHASER'S RESPONSIBILITIES?

Quite a number of problems associated with a product's quality are usually the fault of the purchaser! Obviously the purchaser can only expect to get what he ordered. It is, therefore, extremely important that the actual order is not only correct, but also provides the manufacturer or service provider with all the relevant (and accurate) information required to complete the task.

There is little point in trying to blame the manufacturer or service provider when the finished product doesn't come up to expectation because of an unsatisfactory specification provided by the purchaser. In certain cases (for example when the requirements of the item cannot easily be described in words), it could be very helpful if the purchaser was to provide a drawing as a form of graphic order. In such cases, this drawing should contain all the relevant details such as type of material to be used, the material's grade or condition, the specifications that are to be followed and, where possible, the graphic order/drawing should be to scale.

Figure 8.1 Insufficient information from the purchaser!

Figure 8.2 A good specification provided by the purchaser

If this approach proves impractical, then the order would have to include all the relevant dimensional data, sizes, tolerances etc., or refer to one of the accepted standards.

Having said all that, it must be appreciated that the actual specification being used is also very important for it sets the level of quality required and, therefore, directly affects the price of the article. Clearly, if specifications are too demanding then the final cost of the article will be too high. If specifications are too vague or obscure, then the manufacturer will have difficulty in assembling the object or may even be unable to get it to work correctly.

The choice of manufacturer or supplier of a service is equally important. It is an unfortunate fact of life that purchasers usually consider that the price of the article is the prime and (in some cases), even the only consideration. Buying cheaply is obviously **not** the answer because if a purchaser accepts the lowest offer all too often he will find that delivery times are lengthened (because the manufacturer/supplier can make more profit on other orders), the article produced does not satisfy his requirements and worst of all, the quality of the article is so poor that he has to replace the device well before its anticipated life cycle has been completed.

If a manufacturer or service provider has received official recognition that the quality of his work is up to a particular standard, then the purchaser has a reasonable guarantee that the article being produced will be of a reasonable quality – always assuming that the initial order was correct! Official recognition is taken to mean that an organisation has been assessed and certified to a recognised quality standard such as ISO 9001. In other words he can **prove** his level of quality.

9 WHAT ARE THE SUPPLIER'S RESPONSIBILITIES?

The term 'supplier' normally relates to organisations that manufacture goods **or** provide services. The suppliers prime responsibility must always be to ensure that anything **and everything** leaving their organisation conforms to the specific requirements of the purchaser – particularly with regard to quality.

The simplest way of doing this is for the supplier to ensure that their particular office, production facility or manufacturing/service outlet fully complies with the requirements of the quality standards adopted by the country in which they are manufacturing and the country to whom they intend supplying the component, equipment or system.

To do this they must of course first be aware of the standards applicable to that country, know how to obtain copies of these standards, how to adapt them to their own particular environment and how to get them accepted by the relevant authorities.

Every country has its own set of recognised quality management standards to which suppliers can be assessed and certified. Table 9.1 indicates the most frequently used certification and guideline standards used within the UK.

Although a firm can set out to abide by accepted standards, however, unless they achieve this aim they will fail in their attempt to become a recognised supplier of quality goods. The main points that they should note are:

- that all managerial staff, from the most junior to the most senior, must firmly believe in the importance of quality control and quality assurance and understand how to implement them;
- that managerial staff **must** create an atmosphere in which quality assurance rules are obeyed and not simply avoided just because they are inconvenient, time consuming, laborious or just too boring to bother with;

Table 9.1 Certification and guideline standards

Certification Standards	Description	Guideline Standards	Description
ISO 9001: 2000	Model for quality assurance requirements in design, development, production, installation and servicing	ISO 9004: 2000	Quality management and quality system guidance
ISO 14001: 1996	Requirements for an environmental management system ensuring continual improvement	BS 7799: 1995	Information security management Code of Practice
Investors in People	Model for human resources, with special emphasis on management system requirements for training		

- that there has to be an accepted training scheme to ensure that all members of the firm are regularly brought up to date with the ongoing and the latest requirements of quality assurance;
- that there must be a quality assurance team available to oversee and make sure that quality control and quality assurance are carried out at all times and **at all levels**, within their premises.

Figure 9.1 If you've got it, flaunt it!

In addition, the supplier will have to provide proof that they are supplying a quality product. This is actually a measurement of their quality control and usually takes the form of a suppliers evaluation, surveillance and audit. The evaluation is carried out by:

- the prospective purchaser of the product, or
- an accredited body (such as LRQA, BSI or SGS etc.) which, if success-ful, will allow the supplier to proudly display a compliance certificate and to use the recognised quality mark on their stationery and marketing literature.

10 WHAT TO DO ONCE THE QMS IS ESTABLISHED

So you have finally managed to set up your management system, got everyone working in accordance with it and are starting to reap the benefits of having a consistent approach to doing business. You could be excused to think that all the hard work is over. This is far from the truth, as we already know that ISO 9001:2000 calls for the continual improvement of the management system.

In the following sections we will look at the activities you should carry out once you have set up your QMS.

10.1 Continual improvement

In Section 5.5 we learnt that continual improvement is one of the eight principles of sound management practice. This principle requires a closer look, as any business that fails to improve will ultimately be left behind by the competition. Consider this, you may well have invented the hour glass,

Figure 10.1 Continual improvement keeps you ahead

but there is always someone prepared to progress the design a little further. Resting on your laurels is not an option!

In the past, many companies who attained ISO 9001 certification did not seek to improve their QMS. After the initial enthusiasm of attaining the award, a degree of apathy set in and bad habits re-emerged. It was possible to ignore the QMS until the next assessment was due. This in turn resulted in a decline in standards between assessments and a knee-jerk reaction and subsequent panic was then required to bring the system back up to an acceptable level.

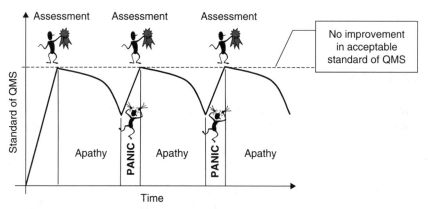

Figure 10.2 The Apathy–Panic cycle!

This approach to retaining the certificate does not instil confidence in your QMS. Neither does it encourage you to seek ways in which to do things better. In short your business processes become stagnant.

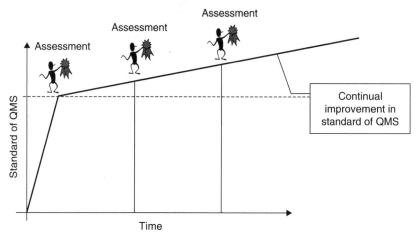

Figure 10.3 The quest for perfection

The only way in which a business will maintain viability and remain competitive is to continually refine the way in which it works. Continual improvement avoids the Apathy–Panic cycle and aims to keep a business in business. It is a never-ending quest for perfection.

Seeking utopia is all well and good but it is not always easy to see where to find it. Your QMS may seem perfect for your purposes and improvements appear impossible to find. So where to start looking?

There is an old adage that says if you can't measure it, you can't manage it. This is especially true of a process driven QMS. By measuring the performance of processes you will see how they are performing and whether they should be improved.

10.2 Process metrics

Just about every process can be measured to see how it is performing. Take for example the process of waking up. The purpose of this process is to wake someone up. So the obvious measure (or metric) would be the number of times the sleeping person responded to the alarm clock by getting out of bed.

Now supposing you set a benchmark or target to this metric, by saying an acceptable standard would be the man getting up on time for 80% of each month. By monitoring his actions over an extended period you would be able to establish whether this target is being met.

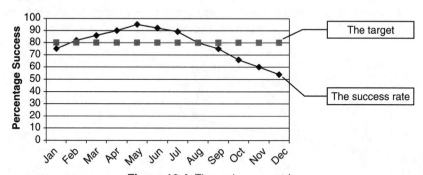

Figure 10.4 The wake up metric

In the above example, it can be seen that this target is not met during the winter months. This therefore represents an opportunity for process improvement. Maybe this would be through altering the process inputs; such as re-defining the time he goes to bed, altering the bedroom temperature or the volume of the alarm. In this way the process is refined to better achieve its intended goal.

This is a very simple example but it demonstrates that processes can be measured and, if necessary improved upon. Of course once a process is refined you must continue to monitor the metrics to establish whether the process has indeed been improved.

10.3 Process improvement tools

There are many tools available to help in targeting and implementing process improvements. The one currently in the ascendancy and showing no signs of losing its popularity is known as Six-Sigma. To be more precise, Six-Sigma is a carefully packaged collection of tools (a toolbox), which can be applied as appropriate to the process being considered.

Six-Sigma tools and techniques are numerous but all have one ultimate goal, that being the improvement of business processes.

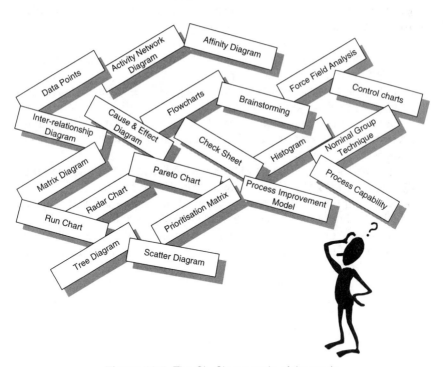

Figure 10.5 The Six-Sigma tools of the trade

Six-Sigma is a far-ranging subject about which numerous books have been written and *ISO 9001:2000 in Brief* could not possibly do it justice. Suffice to say that it is a problem solving methodology that focuses on the measurement of processes, subsequent identification and elimination or control of the root causes of defects/errors and the institutionalisation of improvements within the management system.

For those of you with a mathematical bent it aims to reduce defects to 3.4 in every 1 million. Put another way your product or service is 99.99966% perfect!

Six-Sigma is frowned upon by some Quality Managers; however, the tools are only developments of those used by Quality Managers since the early days of formal business management controls using statistical techniques (*circa* 1920). The tools have simply been better structured and used in a more systematic and logical sequence. Six-Sigma can live quite happily in companies who already embrace ISO standards of business management. Indeed, it has potential to become the key contributor to the continual improvement culture required by ISO 9001:2000.

Experience shows that companies who utilise Six-Sigma as part of their continual improvement strategy not only become more efficient, but also have fewer problems attaining ISO 9001:2000 certification.

For those who are sceptical, Six-Sigma is an invaluable tool in satisfying the following clauses of ISO 9001:2000:

- 4.1 (e) Monitoring, measurement and analysis of processes are all well covered by a Six-Sigma approach.
- 5.4.1 Six-Sigma's statistical analysis will greatly assist in identifying and setting of quality objectives.
- 5.6.2 (c) Management reviews rely heavily on information derived from process metrics. Here again, Six-Sigma will help to deliver the necessary data.
- 7.1 (d) Six-Sigma can be used to generate the records needed to prove the effectiveness of processes; usually in the form of metrics.
- 8.2.3 Perhaps the most important part of Six-Sigma lies in its ability to monitor and measure processes and flag up where they are failing.
- 8.4 Analysis of data. The statistical and evaluation tools within Six-Sigma have been specifically developed over many years to accurately analyse data.
- 8.5.1 ISO 9001:2000 is very clear on the need for continual improvement. As already mentioned, the inclusion of Six-Sigma within a management system will go a long way to satisfying this clause.
- 8.5.2 Corrective action can readily be distilled from Six-Sigma methodologies.
- 8.5.3 Preventive action can be identified through using Six-Sigma 'what if' analysis, which highlights potential problems.

It can be seen that Six-Sigma really can support any business management system by satisfying that age-old adage of 'if you can't measure it, you can't manage it'. To this end ISO 9001 and Six-Sigma can be considered mutually beneficial to a business.

10.3.1 How do I apply Six-Sigma to improve my processes?

Six-Sigma uses the 'IMAIC' problem-solving model. IMAIC stands for Identify, Measure, Analyse, Improve, and Control. Each phase is summarised below:

Identify. This phase aims at pinpointing those processes that are causing your company problems. Management will also define the requirements for each process, i.e. set the standard to be expected.

Measure. This phase gathers data to establish the current level of process performance.

Analyse. This is where the root cause of the problem is identified through the critical analysis of process metric data.

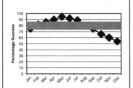

Improve revolves around developing and testing ways in which the process can be improved.

Control is simply putting in place whatever means are needed to keep the refined process in check. This could be through defining upper and lower tolerances, inspection requirements, methods of monitoring, etc.

Keep between the lines!

10.3.2 Why have six Sigmas, when one would do?

For those of you with a mathematical bent, 'Sigma' is the value of the process standard deviation for a given characteristic.

In simpler terms consider an archery target. The 'given characteristic' would be the bull's-eye, because this is ultimately what you want to achieve. Fire a few arrows at the target and see how scattered they are from the bull's-eye. The greater the spread, the larger the standard deviation.

The term Sigma Level refers to how many standard deviations fit between the mean (the target) and the specification limits (the edges of the target). Therefore, a process with a smaller standard deviation will be able to fit more Sigma Levels into the same distance as a process with a large standard deviation. The higher the Sigma Level, the better the quality of the product or service, i.e. the more arrows hitting the bull's-eye.

The table below displays various Sigma Levels in terms of defects per million activities. An archer with a Sigma Level of 6 would be an ideal Olympic champion, as only three of his 1,000,000 arrows would ever miss the bull's-eye!

Table 10.1 Six is the best!

Sigma Level	Defects per million	% Yield
1	691,463	30.854
2	308,538	69.146
3	66,807	93.319
4	6.210	99.379
5	233	99.977
6	3.4	99.99966

10.4 Audit

Audit – *'Systematic, independent and documented process for obtaining audit evidence and evaluating it objectively to determine the extent to which audit criteria are fulfilled'* (ISO 9000:2000)

Having set up your management system and implemented appropriate process metrics you could be excused to think that this will provide you with sufficient confidence that everything within your business is functioning properly. This is not the case, as you still have no idea where the strengths and weaknesses lie in your management system. This is where auditing can be used as a means of establishing whether:

- your management system is being used as it was originally intended;
- there are areas in the system which could be improved.

One other incentive for implementing an internal audit process is that ISO 9001:2000 requires it as a mandatory documented procedure.

Auditing is all about checking that you conform to predetermined requirements (i.e. you do what you say you do!). For example, if you state in a process that staff must wear hard hats to perform a particularly dangerous job and a safety auditor visits a site only to discover they are all wearing flat caps, then your process is not being followed. The auditor will ensure that hard hats are worn, by issuing a non-conformance.

Figure 10.6 Auditing is good for you!

This is a particularly good example of how an auditor can maintain discipline within a workforce and ensures that your management system is being adhered to. The auditor may also have saved someone's life, not to mention the costs of an accident claim.

Auditing generally follows a linear process starting with establishing the criteria against which you are auditing and leading to a report concluding whether the criteria is being met. Should the audit find problems with the performance of a process, then you will implement corrective action aimed at preventing reoccurrence. A simple process map of the internal audit procedure is shown in the next figure.

Remember, auditing is not a witch-hunt aimed at finding fault with people. Where things go wrong it is usually the fault of the process, not the person performing it.

There are three generic categories of audit, which you may come across:

- **First party.** Also known as internal auditing, where (as the name suggests) members of a business look inwards at their own processes. This

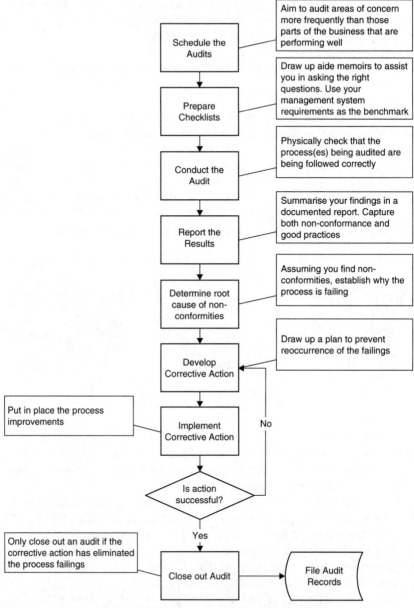

Figure 10.7 A generic audit process

is the least effective form of auditing, as generally the auditors will find it difficult to criticise their own work. To minimise this, it is desirable to get staff to audit each other's processes, thereby instilling a degree of independence.

- **Second party.** These are audits carried out by your customers to satisfy themselves you are capable of doing a job and are generally referred to as Vendor Audits.
- **Third party.** Personnel who are neither staff working within your business or your customers will carry out this type of audit. So who are they? Generally these are employees of accredited certification bodies. These bodies are the companies who audit your business and, if found to be compliant, certify you to ISO 9001:2000.

In addition to the three categories of audit, there are many types of audit that can be used to measure conformance to ISO 9001:2000:

- **System Audits.** Carried out to ensure a business management system is sufficiently comprehensive to control all of the activities within that business. Generally, this type of audit would look for gaps in the management system that may result in them not achieving their business objectives.
- **Process Audits.** Focuses specifically on single processes to verify if they are capable of delivering the outputs expected of them.
- **Management Audits.** Checks carried out to see if the strategic plan of the business reflects their business objectives and more specifically whether they have met the requirements of the intended market.

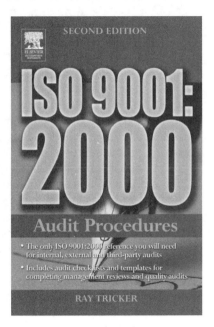

These are but a few audit types. Further details can be sought in Ray Tricker's book on the subject, *ISO 9001:2000 Audit Procedures,* 2nd edn.

10.5 Certification

In this book you have so far learnt about setting up an ISO 9001: 2000 compliant management system. Now you could stop there in the knowledge that your business is a lot better off because of it. But for those companies who want to go the extra mile you can seek to gain third-party certification to the actual standard. This certificate is the tangible proof that your company operates to the exacting standards of ISO 9001:2000.

In this section you will learn the basics of how to go about obtaining certification.

Certificates are awarded by accredited Certification Bodies (also known as Registrars). Be warned, not all companies who profess being able to award ISO 9001:2000 certificates are accredited. To find out who are certified within the UK you will need to contact the United Kingdom Accreditation Service (UKAS).

American National Standards Institute

Within the USA, the American National Standards Institute accredits Certification Bodies. Contact details can be found at the rear of this book.

The cost of certification can vary significantly as Certification Bodies have different pricing structures. Some will charge for each and every visit, assessment and follow-up surveillance inspections. Others may be happy to settle for a one off fixed payment to take you through the certification process, followed by an annual renewal fee. When considering a suitable Certification Body you should obtain a number of quotes to establish the best offer.

The amount of time you need to attain certification is dependent upon a number of variables including the size of the company, the complexity of its business processes, the resources available to develop the QMS, etc. It would be very unfair to suggest any minimum time scale from starting to develop the QMS to finally receiving the certificate. However, do not be fooled into thinking it is a quick exercise. Experience shows that for most small and medium enterprises allowing one year is not unreasonable. However, some larger companies have been known to attain certification in considerably less time, but this is usually down to the employment of a dedicated quality development team.

Rest assured that however long it takes you it will be well worthwhile.

Certification Bodies do not generally provide a consultancy service so it is desirable to use an independent consultant to ease the way through the certification process. You could of course do it yourself, but there are pitfalls that an experienced consultant would help you over (and potentially save you money by avoiding unnecessary repeat visits from the Certification Body).

The process map shown on the following page gives a very basic sequence of the events you should go through before considering contacting a Certified Body.

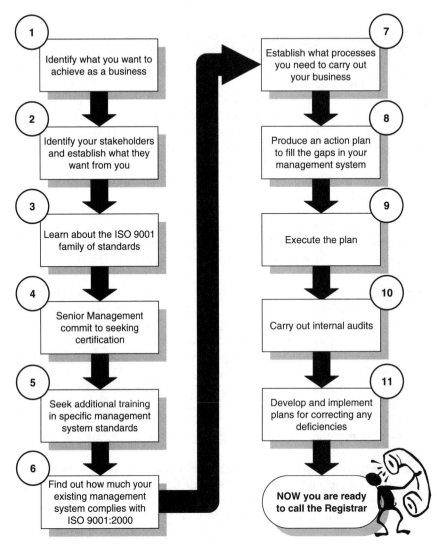

Figure 10.8 Getting the QMS up and running

Notes:

(1) Establish your mission, what the business is all about and most importantly what your goals are for installing a management system, e.g.
boost your profits, reduce waste, improve staff morale, refine your production methods, etc.

(2) Your business has many stakeholders. Consider not just your customers, but your staff, shareholders, the environment, subcontractors,
etc. Also try and establish what each stakeholder expects from you.

(3) You cannot put in an ISO 9001:2000 compliant management system
without some knowledge on the subject (that is probably why you
bought this book!). Seek advice, employ a consultant or recruit a quality professional into your team.

(4) The most fundamental decision any head of a business must make.
Without senior management commitment the initiative is bound to fail.
If the bosses are not interested in developing a compliant management system then no amount of persuasion by the staff will make any
difference.

(5) We have learnt that there are many types of management system
standards intended for specific purposes. Get yourself trained up in
those that apply. For example, you may be a company offering project
management services. In that case ISO 10006 would apply.

(6) This is termed a gap analysis and as the name suggests you will be
looking for any holes in your existing management system that need
filling in order to become compliant to the standard. This could be
carried out by a consultant or internally.

(7) Identify and draw up those processes/procedures that are critical to
making your business a success. Don't forget those mandatory ones
demanded by the standard.

(8) Planning how you intend closing out the gaps in your system is vital to
ensure you do not overlook anything. You will also have to consider
how you will manage the changes into your business.

(9) Implement the plan and introduce your fully compliant management
system.

(10) You may be very keen to get the third party assessor in, but hold back
for at least three months to give a chance for the system to bed down
and for internal audits to be carried out to establish if everything is
basically performing as it should. This will also give you a chance to
put any non-conformances right.

(11) **NOW** you can call the assessor in.

In the following figure you will see a typical route to certification. Once you
are comfortable that your management system is ready for assessment
and have chosen a suitable Certification Body, the process continues normally through a two stage assessment. Not every Certified Body follows
this convention, but on the whole the principles remain the same.

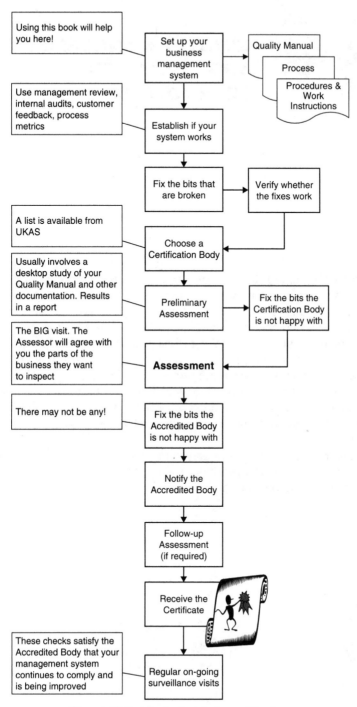

Figure 10.9 A typical route to certification
Good Luck!

11 QUALITY MANAGEMENT AND COMPUTER TECHNOLOGY

Nowadays, computer technology appears in just about every walk of life and in most instances provides great benefits. Quality Management is no exception to this rule as computers offer significant advantages when implementing and controlling a Quality Management System.

One of the most onerous tasks a Quality Manager has to do is to maintain the Quality Manual. Now if there is only one manual this is not much of a problem. Difficulties arise when there are numerous copies of the manual dotted around the business, all of which need to be controlled to ensure their content is current. This problem is further compounded when a business is spread throughout a country or in the case of multi-nationals throughout the world.

The same problems arise when you need a number of isolated personnel to perform the same process. It is very difficult to ensure that everyone has the same version to work from.

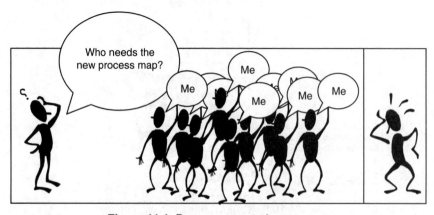

Figure 11.1 Document control gone crazy

This is where computer technology comes into its own. Through the use of a company Intranet it is possible for the Quality Manager to:

• Maintain one centrally located management system;
• Permit all personnel access to the same information;
• Control only one set of documents.

It is clear that such a system is very efficient and hence cost effective. So what is a company Intranet? Put crudely it is like a mini version of the World Wide Web, except that only your staff can access the website. So, by turning the contents of your Quality Manual into an Intranet website all your personnel can access the current version.

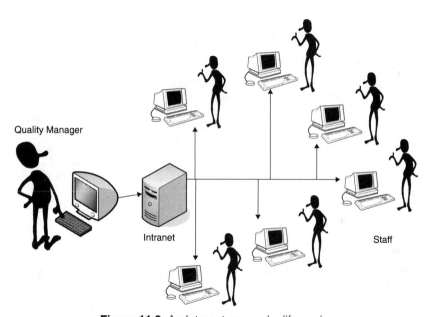

Figure 11.2 An Intranet can make life easier

Computers are therefore ideal as a means of control and distribution of processes, procedures and work instructions. They are also an ideal means of producing and then seamlessly combining your process maps. There are any number of software packages offering process mapping capabilities. Indeed, Microsoft's own Visio® package is more than adequate for most purposes, although you can purchase bespoke software should you have more specific needs.

By using process mapping software it is possible to set up standard templates to ensure your maps all have a consistent appearance and convention. This is of importance if you are getting a number of personnel to draw up processes.

You will recall from the chapter on Quality Processes that they are often complex and require a number of levels to fully detail the activities. This can result in problems finding the way between the maps, especially when they are in paper form. By converting your process maps into web pages it is possible to include electronic links. This is called 'hyperlinking' and enables separate processes to be connected and hence aids navigation between them.

In the following diagram you will see by attaching hyperlinks between points on different process maps it is possible to jump between them and consequently maintain continuity and the sequence of processes.

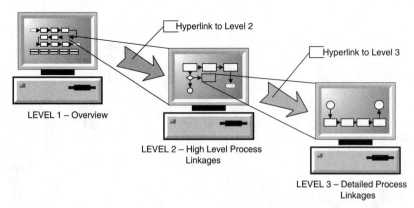

Figure 11.3 Hyperlinked process maps

One other area where computers come into their own is for communication. ISO 9001:2000 requires senior management to ensure that appropriate communication processes are established within the organisation and that communication takes place regarding the effectiveness of the Quality Management System. What better way than using your office email facility.

Consider also the possibility that you may need to have current versions of legislation made available to your personnel. Yet again the centralisation of this documentation within an Intranet will avoid unnecessary duplication.

In summary computers can greatly assist quality management in the following areas:

- Centrally managing one master copy of the Quality Manual;
- Document distribution;
- Document control;
- Process map development;
- Process map navigation through hyperlinking;

- Communicating quality issues;
- Centrally storing master copies of applicable specifications, standards and legislation.

In other words, computers make you more efficient and efficiency means lower costs.

When developing your QMS serious consideration should be given to the use of computer technology. The days of paper-based systems are numbered. Computers will make your life a whole lot easier.

Figure 11.4 A computer is a Quality Manager's friend

Annex A – ISO 9001:2000 – A summary of requirements

Note: Bold text denotes a mandatory procedure.

Section of ISO 9001:2000	Title of Section	Intent of Clauses
4	Quality Management System	
4.1	General Requirements	You are required to have a business management system, developed and implemented through: • identifying the processes used to carry out your business; • determining the sequence of these processes; • establishing ways to ensure that the processes are carried out correctly; • ensuring that you have adequate and appropriate resources; • showing that you monitor and improve your system.
4.2	Documentation Requirements	
4.2.1	General	The following documentation must be included in the management system: • quality Policy and Quality Objectives; • a Quality Manual; • the documented procedures required by the standard (see bold text for mandatory procedures); • the records required by the standard to prove that you meet its requirements.
4.2.2	Quality Manual	You must have an up to date Quality Manual, which addresses the following: • the scope of the management system;

Section of ISO 9001:2000	Title of Section	Intent of Clauses
		• those parts of the standard that do not apply to your organisation, including justification. NOTE – Only those requirements in Section 7 can be excluded; • the documented procedures that are required by ISO 9000 (see bold text); • a description of how your business processes interact.
4.2.3	**Control of Documents**	A process must be in place that ensures only the correct version of documents is in use. These documents must be reviewed and approved prior to use. You should also have a record of what documents exist and which version is the correct one. You must periodically review them for ongoing fitness for purpose.
4.2.4	**Control of Records**	You must keep records to prove that you are operating your management system correctly. Records must be kept for a predetermined period, in good condition and be readily retrievable. The procedure will state storage requirements.
5	Management Responsibility	
5.1	Management Commitment	You shall: • define the commitment of your senior management to the development and improvement of the system; • have a Quality Policy; • define Quality Objectives; • conduct management reviews; • ensure that sufficient resources are available.
5.2	Customer Focus	Senior management shall define their commitment to determining, meeting and enhancing customer satisfaction. How they intend doing this should be explained.

Section of ISO 9001:2000	Title of Section	Intent of Clauses
5.3	Quality Policy	You must have a Quality Policy pertinent to your products/services. The Quality Policy provides the focus of your quality system and is the very top document of the management system (unless you also have a Mission Statement). Your policy must include a process for establishing and reviewing Quality Objectives.
5.4	Planning	
5.4.1	Quality Objectives	You must make sure that you have defined your objectives for quality, using measurable terms. These objectives must align with your Quality Policy.
5.4.2	Quality Management System Planning	You must ensure that you have planned and identified your objectives for the Quality Management System. When changes are made to your system, you must also ensure that the integrity of the system is maintained such that your system continues to meet the requirements of ISO 9001:2000.
5.5	Responsibility, Authority & Communication	
5.5.1	Responsibility & authority	You must define and communicate out the roles and responsibilities of the key functions within your organisation, so that personnel understand who does what.
5.5.2	Management Representative	Senior management shall nominate a person responsible for: • ensuring that the quality management processes are installed;

Section of ISO 9001:2000	Title of Section	Intent of Clauses
		• reporting performance of the management system; • promoting awareness of customer requirements. This person must be a member of your management.
5.5.3	Internal Communication	Adequate communication shall be put in place (between the various levels of staff) to facilitate a two-way dialogue on the effectiveness of the management system.
5.6	Management Review	
5.6.1	General	You must review the function of the quality system to ensure that it is current and effective. The review must also embrace opportunities for improvement.
5.6.2	Review Input	The inputs for the review must include: • audit results; • customer feedback; • process & product performance/ conformity; • status of preventive/corrective actions; • follow-up actions from previous management reviews; • changes that could affect the management system; • recommendations for improvement.
5.6.3	Review Output	The outcome of the review shall include actions and decisions on: • improvement of the effectiveness of the management system; • improvement of the product (or service); • resources needs (i.e. what resources you require to achieve these improvements).

Section of ISO 9001:2000	Title of Section	Intent of Clauses
6	Resource Management	
6.1	Provision of Resources	You must provide adequate resources to implement, maintain and improve the management system and enhance customer satisfaction.
6.2	Human Resources	
6.2.1	General	You must ensure that you have competent, trained/experienced staff.
6.2.2	Competence, Awareness & Training	You must: • define the skills required to perform tasks which affect product quality; • provide training; • evaluate the effectiveness of the training; • ensure personnel are aware of the importance of their tasks; • keep records of the training and experience.
6.3	Infrastructure	You must provide facilities (in the form of buildings, workspace, tools & equipment, supporting services, etc.) that will ensure the product/service conforms to your customers' requirements.
6.4	Work Environment	You must determine and manage the environmental factors needed to achieve product/service conformity.
7	Product Realisation	
7.1	Planning of Product Realisation	You must: • determine the Quality Objectives and requirements for your products; • ensure that you plan all of the processes needed to provide your products/services;

Section of ISO 9001:2000	Title of Section	Intent of Clauses
		• plan the required inspection/testing (V&V) activities; • identify what records must be retained to provide evidence that the product conforms to requirements.
7.2	Customer-related Processes	
7.2.1	Determination of Requirements Related to the Product	You must establish and, if needs be, clarify what your customer expects you to deliver and any obligations that arise from it, such as statutory requirements to be met.
7.2.2	Review of Requirements Related to the Product	Product requirements must be defined and reviewed prior to committing to supply. You will ensure contract issues are resolved and that you have the necessary resources to deliver. The review shall be recorded. Where a customer does not provide written requirements you shall confirm your interpretation of their needs prior to acceptance of the order. You must define how changes in requirements are recorded and how the information is circulated around the relevant sections of your organisation.
7.2.3	Customer Communication	You must identify lines of communication between the customer and your organisation with regard to product information, enquiries and contract amendments, feedback including complaints, etc.
7.3	Design and Development	
7.3.1	Design & Development Planning	You shall determine the various design/development processes and any review, verification & validation stages. Responsibilities and authorities shall also be defined.

Section of ISO 9001:2000	Title of Section	Intent of Clauses
7.3.2	Design & Development Inputs	Design inputs shall be defined (i.e. the information needed to design or develop the product or service). Your inputs will include any relevant functional requirements, standards, legal requirements (e.g. mandatory safety requirements, packaging disposal/recycling requirements, CE marking requirements, etc.). Where pertinent, previous designs should be considered. Design inputs must be reviewed for adequacy, be complete, clear and not conflict with each other.
7.3.3	Design & Development Outputs	Design (& development) outputs, such as drawings, reports, etc. shall be produced such that they can be checked for compliance against design inputs. Outputs shall also provide information for purchasing, product acceptance criteria and characteristics that are essential for its safe and proper use.
7.3.4	Design & Development Review	Design activities must be reviewed at appropriate stages to evaluate whether they will meet requirements. These can include modelling, prototype tests, beta testing, etc. The review will include the identification and recording of any problems and follow-up actions. The review plan should identify at what stages these reviews will occur. Records must be kept.
7.3.5	Design & Development Verification	Design outputs must be verified to ensure that the design meets the input requirements. Verification shall be planned and recorded.
7.3.6	Design & Development Validation	The finished product or service shall be validated to check that it is capable of carrying out its intended role. Validation shall be planned and recorded.

Section of ISO 9001:2000	Title of Section	Intent of Clauses
7.3.7	Control of Design & Development Changes	Design changes must be reviewed and recorded. The effect of design changes on any sections of the design work already completed must be considered.
7.4	Purchasing	
7.4.1	Purchasing Process	You must ensure that purchased products conform to the requirements you specified. You will also ensure that you select, through evaluation, suitable suppliers.
7.4.2	Purchasing Information	Contracts and purchase orders must clearly state what you require, including if necessary, product approval requirements, supplier qualifications and management system requirements. Purchasing information must be reviewed for adequacy before it is sent to the supplier.
7.4.3	Verification of Purchased Product	Perhaps better understood as goods inwards inspection. You are expected to define and implement those inspections needed to satisfy yourself that the delivered product meets your specified requirements.
7.5	Production & Service Provision	
7.5.1	Control of Production & Service Provision	Processes that are needed to deliver your product or service need to be controlled. These controls, which need to be planned and implemented, include: • information that describes the characteristics of the product (so that inspections and tests can be conducted); • work instructions to define 'key-stroke' operations expected of a member of staff;

Section of ISO 9001:2000	Title of Section	Intent of Clauses
		• providing appropriate equipment; • availability and use of suitable monitoring and measuring devices; • product release and delivery criteria.
7.5.2	Validation of Processes for Production & Service Provision	Previously known as hidden processes, i.e. those processes that produce items that cannot be tested directly and consequently require tighter control through: • the review and approval of such processes; • approval of equipment and personnel; • defining procedures must be followed when producing the product/service; • defining what records must be retained; • revalidation criteria.
7.5.3	Identification and Traceability	Where appropriate you must identify materials and goods to allow for traceability. Not everything needs to be traceable, but consideration should be given to identifying items which could easily be mixed up or confused, or where proof of calibration to national standards is required.
7.5.4	Customer Property	Customers occasionally supply their own products for example, to incorporate into a system. Where this occurs you must identify, verify, protect and safeguard it. Furthermore, if you break or lose it then this must be reported to the customer and records kept.
7.5.5	Preservation of Product	You must ensure that processes exist to ensure the safe identification, handling, packaging, storage and preservation of all materials and finished products. These safeguards include delivery to the intended destination.

Section of ISO 9001:2000	Title of Section	Intent of Clauses
7.6	Control of Monitoring & Measuring Devices	Monitoring & measuring is vital to check that a product (or service) meets predetermined requirements. Processes need to be established that will prove that you have indeed met the intended specification. The equipment used to carry out monitoring and measuring will need to be calibrated, identified, safeguarded from adjustment and protected from damage. Where equipment has been found to be out of calibration you are required to have a mechanism in place to intercept the affected product (e.g. product recall).
8	Measurement, Analysis & Improvement	
8.1	General	You must plan and implement your monitoring, measuring, analysis and improvement activities, in order to demonstrate your product conforms to requirements, your management system conforms to ISO 9001 and to improve your processes/procedures. You will need to consider the statistical techniques and other methods needed to achieve this requirement.
8.2	Monitoring & Measurement	
8.2.1	Customer Satisfaction	ISO 9001:2000 is customer focused. It is vital therefore that you monitor customer satisfaction through preplanned and defined methods. The resulting information is utilised during management review.
8.2.2	**Internal Audit**	Internal auditing is a mandatory requirement aimed at determining whether the management system conforms to the planned arrangements you have detailed in section 7.1 and

Section of ISO 9001:2000	Title of Section	Intent of Clauses
		also to ISO 9001:2000. The audit programme shall be planned, with frequency and extent being based on the importance of the processes to be audited. The written procedure shall identify responsibilities and ensure that non-conformities are actioned without undue delay.
8.2.3	Monitoring & Measuring of Processes	You are required to have methods in place for ensuring that your processes are suitable and remain so. This will include the actions to be taken when a process is not delivering expected results.
8.2.4	Monitoring & Measuring of Product	You are required to monitor and measure the product or service at appropriate stages. Records must be retained that identify the person who released the goods or services at the predetermined hold points. A product must not be released until all of the required actions have been conducted.
8.3	**Control of Non-conforming Product**	You must have a written procedure to ensure that non-conforming products (i.e. sub-standard, damaged, etc.) are not used or delivered accidentally. Non-conforming products can be dealt with in any one of three ways: • removal of the defect, in which case it needs to be reverified against the original specification; • authorising its use under concession; • preventing its use. These actions should be recorded.
8.4	Analysis of Data	Your organisation shall collect and analyse sufficient data to demonstrate the effectiveness of the management system. The analysis will identify where improvements can be made.

Section of ISO 9001:2000	Title of Section	Intent of Clauses
		Data shall include information relating to customer satisfaction, product conformity, process trends and suppliers.
8.5	Improvement	
8.5.1	Continual Improvement	You are required to continually improve your management system through the results obtained from data analysis, audit results, management review, corrective/preventive actions, etc.
8.5.2	**Corrective Action**	Inevitably things will go wrong from time to time and you should identify, record, investigate and fix them. The intention being to prevent them occurring again. A written procedure must capture your intentions. You must also review the corrective action to see if it has been effective.
8.5.3	**Preventive Action**	Using suitable methodology you must attempt to predict the causes of potential non-conformities and implement action to prevent them occurring. NOTE – Risk Assessment is more desirable than a crystal ball! As with corrective actions you must have a procedure and record the results of actions taken and review the effect of preventive action.

ABBREVIATIONS AND ACRONYMS

ACE	Allied Command Europe
AECMA	Association Europeen des Constructeurs de Materiel Aerospatial
AFNOR	Association Français de Normalisation
AMIQA	Associate Member of the Institute of Quality Assurance
ANSI	American National Standards Institute
AQAP	Allied Quality Assurance Publications (NATO)
AS 9000	Quality system standard for the aerospace industry, issued by SAE (USA)
ASQ	American Society for Quality (was ASQC)
ASQC	American Society for Quality Control (now ASQ)
BEC	British Electro-Technical Committee (part of BSI)
BS	British Standard, issued by BSI
BSI	British Standards Institution
CASCO	Committee for Conformity Assessment
CCA	Accord de Certification du CENELEC (CENELEC Certification Agreement)
CCIR	International Radio Consultative Committee
CCITT	The International Telegraph and Telephony Consultative Committee
CD	Committee Draft
CECC	CENELEC Electronic Components Committee
CEE	International Commission on rules for the approval of Electrical Equipment (now mostly replaced by IEC publications)
CEN	Commission European de Normalisation
CENELEC	European Committee for Electrotechnical Standardisation

COMSEC	Communications Security
CSA	Canadian Standards Association
DEF	Defence Standard (UK)
Def Spec	Defence Specification (UK)
DEF STAN	Defence Standards (UK)
DIN	Deutsches Institut für Normung (German Institute for Standardisation)
DIS	Draft International Standard
DTI	Department of Trade and Industry
DOD	(American) Division of Defence
EEC	European Economic Community
EFQM	European Foundation for Quality Management
EFTA	European Free Trade Association (Iceland, Norway, Switzerland and Liechtenstein)
EN	European Number (for European standards)
EN HD	European Harmonised Directive
EOQ	European Organisation for Quality
EOQC	European Organisation for Quality Control (now EOQ)
EQFM	European Foundation of Quality Management
ERRI	European Rail Research Institute
ERTMS	European Rail Traffic Management System
ETCS	European Train Control System
ETSI	European Telecommunications Standards Institute
EU	European Union
FDIS	Final Draft International Standard
FIIE(elec)	Fellow of the Institution of Electronics and Electrical Incorporated Engineers
FinstM	Fellow of the Institute of Management
IAF	International Accreditation Forum
IEC	International Electrotechnical Commission
IECC	International Electrotechnical Commission Council
IECQ	IEC Quality Assessment System for Electronic Components
IEE	Institution of Electrical Engineers
IQA	Institute of Quality Assurance
ISO	International Organisation for Standardisation
ISO/TC176	The ISO Technical Committee responsible for the ISO 9000 series of standards
IT	Information Technology
ITU	International Telecommunications Union
JPL	Jet Propulsion Laboratory

LAN	Local Area Network
Mil-Spec	Military Specification (USA)
Mil-Std	Military Standard (USA)
MIQA	Member of the Institute of Quality Assurance
MIRSE	Member of the Institution of Railway Signal Engineers
MOD	Ministry of Defence
MSc	Master of Science
NASA	National Aeronautics and Space Administration
NATO	North Atlantic Treaty Organisation
NSA	National Supervising Authority
NSOQA	National Standards Organisation
QAI	Quality Assurance Inspector
QC	Quality Control
QMS	Quality Management System
QP	Quality Procedure
QS	(automotive standard)
QT	(telecomms standard)
RAMS	Reliability, Availability, Maintenance and Safety
SIS	Swedish Institute for Standards
TC	Technical Committee
TQM	Total Quality Management (e.g. BS 7850)
TTCI	Transportation Technology Center Inc
UIC	Union International des Chemins de fer
UK	United Kingdom
VDE	Verband Deutsch Elektrotechniker
WD	Working Draft
WI	Work Instruction

REFERENCES

Standards

Number	Date	Title
ANSI 90 series		American quality standards
BS 0	1997	A Standard for Standards: Compilation of. Parts 1 to 3
BS 4778	1991	Quality vocabulary
BS 4891	1972	A Guide to Quality Assurance (withdrawn)
BS 5750	1987	Quality systems – Principal concepts and applications. Superseded by ISO 9000:1994
BS 7799	1995	Information security management system code of practice
BS 7850 series	1992	Total quality management
BS 8800	2004	Guide to occupational health and safety management systems
DEF STAN 13-131/2	1997	Ordnance Board safety guidelines for weapons and munitions
ISO 9000	1994 series	Replaced by the ISO 9000:2000 series of standards
ISO 9000	2000	Quality management systems – Fundamentals and vocabulary
ISO 9001	2000	Quality management systems – Requirements

Number	Date	Title
ISO 9004	2000	Quality management systems – Guidance for performance improvement
ISO 10005	1995	Quality management – guidelines for quality plans
ISO 10012	2003	Measurement management systems. Requirements for measurement processes & measuring equipment
ISO/TR 10013	2001	Guidelines for quality management documentation
ISO 14001	1996	Environmental Management Systems – Specifications with guidance for use
ISO 19011	2002	Guidelines for quality and/or environmental management system auditing
QS 9000	1998	Quality system requirements of the automotive industry

NOTES

Extracts from British Standards are reproduced with the permission of the British Standards Institute. Complete copies of all British Standards can be obtained, by post, from Customer Services, BSI Standards, 389 Chiswick High Road, London W4 4AL.

Books by the same author

Title	Details	Publisher
Quality and Standards in Electronics	Ensures that manufacturers are aware of all the UK, European and international necessities, know the current status of these regulations and standards, and where to obtain them.	Butterworth-Heinemann ISBN: 0 7506 2531 7

Title	Details	Publisher
Environmental Requirements for Electro-mechanical and Electronic Equipment	Definitive reference containing all the background guidance, ranges, test specifications, case studies and regulations worldwide.	Butterworth-Heinemann ISBN: 0 7506 3902 4
MDD Compliance using Quality Management Techniques	Easy to follow guide to MDD, enabling purchaser to customise the Quality Management System to suit his own business.	Butterworth-Heinemann ISBN: 0 7506 4441 9
CE Conformity Marking	Essential information for any manufacturer or distributor wishing to trade in the EU.	Butterworth-Heinemann ISBN: 0 7506 4813 9
ISO 9001:2000 for Small Businesses, 3rd edn	Explains the importance of ISO 9001:2000, the ISO 9000:2000 family and helps businesses draw up a quality plan that will allow them to meet the challenges of the marketplace.	Butterworth-Heinemann ISBN: 0 7506 6617 X
Building Regulations in Brief, 2nd edn	Concise guide to the UK Building Regulations for the many people working on simple projects such as building extensions and building adaptations.	Butterworth-Heinemann ISBN: 0 7506 6311 1
ISO 9001:2000 Audit Procedures, 2nd edn	A complete set of audit check sheets and explanations to assist authors in completing internal, external and third part audits of *newly implemented, existing* and *transitional* QMSs	Butterworth-Heinemann ISBN: 0 7506 6615 3
Optoelectronics and Fiber Optics Technology	User friendly guide to technology and applications of fiber optics and optoelectronics	Butterworth-Heinemann ISBN: 0 7506 5370 1

GLOSSARY

Acceptable quality level: A measure of the number of failures that a production process is allowed. Usually expressed as a percentage.

Accreditation: Certification, by a duly recognised body, of facilities, capability, objectivity, competence and integrity of an agency, service or operational group or individual to provide the specific service/s or operation/s as needed.

Assemblies: Several pieces of equipment assembled by a manufacturer to constitute an integrated and functional whole.

Audit: Systematic, independent and documented process for obtaining evidence and evaluating it objectively to determine the extent to which audit criteria are fulfilled.

Audit team: One or more auditors conducting an audit, one of whom is appointed as leader.

CEN (European Committee for Standardisation): European equivalent of ISO.

CENELEC (European Committee for Electrotechnical Standardisation) certification body: An impartial body who have the necessary competence and reliability to operate a certification scheme.

Certification: The procedure and action by a duly authorised body of determining, verifying and attesting in writing to the qualifications of personnel, processes, procedures, or items in accordance with applicable requirements.

Certification body: An impartial body, governmental or non-governmental, possessing the necessary competence and reliability to operate a certification system, and in which the interests of all parties concerned with the functioning of the system are represented. An impartial body who have the necessary competence and reliability to operate a certification scheme.

Chief inspector: An individual who is responsible for the manufacturer's Quality Management System (also referred to as the Quality Manager).

Company: Term used primarily to refer to a business first party, the purpose of which is to supply a product or service.

Compliance: An affirmative indication or judgement that a product or service has met the requirements of the relevant specifications, contract or regulation. Also the state of meeting the requirements.

Conformance: An affirmative indication or judgement that a product or service has met the requirements of the relevant specifications, contract or regulation. Also the state of meeting the requirements.

Contract: Agreed requirements between a supplier and customer transmitted by any means.

Customer: Ultimate consumer, user, client, beneficiary or second party.

Customer satisfaction: Customer's opinion of the degree to which a transaction has met the customer's needs and expectations.

Defect: Non-fulfilment of a requirement related to an intended or specified use.

Design and development: Set of processes that transforms requirements into specified characteristics and into the specification of the product realisation process.

Distributor: An organisation that is contractually authorised by one or more manufacturers to store, repack and sell completely finished components from these manufacturers.

Document: Information and its support medium.

Environment: All of the external physical conditions that may influence the performance of a product or service.

Equipment: Machines, apparatus, fixed or mobile devices, control components and instrumentation thereof and detection or prevention systems which, separately or jointly, are intended for the generation, transfer, storage, measurement, control and conversion of energy for the processing of material and which are capable of causing an explosion through their own potential sources of ignition.

External failure costs: The costs arising outside an organisation after the delivery to customer/user due to failure to fulfil the customer/user quality requirements.

In-process inspection: Inspection carried out at various stages during processing.

QA Inspectors perform these on a random basis or while assisting the technician. They may also be considered as 'Training' inspections and are meant to help the technician perform better maintenance whilst actually learning about the equipment.

International Organisation for Standardisation (ISO): Comprises the national standards bodies of more than 50 countries whose aim is to coordinate the international harmonisation of national standards.

Item: A part, a component, equipment, sub-system or system or defined quantity of material or service that can be individually considered and separately examined or tested.

An actual or conventional object on which a set of observations can be made.

An observed value, either qualitative (attributes) or quantitative (measured).

Maintenance: The combination of technical and administrative actions that are taken to retain or restore an item to a state in which it can perform its stated function.

Management: Co-ordinated activities to direct and control an organisation.

Management system: To establish policy and objectives and to achieve those objectives.

Manufacturer: An organisation, which carries out or controls such stages in the manufacture of electronic components that enable it to accept responsibility for capability approval or qualification approval, inspection and release of electronic components.

Material: A generic term covering equipment, stores, supplies and spares which form the subject of a contract.

Non-conformity: Non-fulfilment of a requirement.

Organisation: Group of people and facilities with an orderly arrangement of responsibilities, authorities and relationships.

A company, corporation, firm or enterprise, whether incorporated or not, public or private.

Organisational structure: Orderly arrangement of responsibilities, authorities and relationships between people.

Procedure: Describes the way to perform an activity or process.

Process inspection: Inspection of a process by examination of the process itself, the product characteristics at the appropriate stage(s) of the process.

Producer's quality costs: The expenditure incurred by the producer associated with prevention and appraisal activities and with the failure to achieve quality requirements during marketing, design and development, procurement, manufacturing, installation and use.

Product: Result of a process.

Note: There are four agreed generic product categories:

- hardware (e.g. engine mechanical part);
- software (e.g. computer program);
- services (e.g. transport);
- processed materials (e.g. lubricant).

Hardware and processed materials are generally tangible products, while software or services are generally intangible.

Most products comprise elements belonging to different generic product categories. Whether the product is then called hardware, processed material, software or service depends on the dominant element.

Project: Unique process, consisting of a set of co-ordinated and controlled activities with start and finish dates, undertaken to achieve an objective conforming to specific requirements, including the constraints of time, costs and resources.

Quality: Ability of a set of inherent characteristics of a product, system or process to fulfil requirements of customers and other interested parties.

The totality of features and characteristics of a product or service that bear upon its ability to satisfy stated or implied needs.

Quality Assurance: Part of quality management, focused on providing confidence that quality requirements are fulfilled.

Quality characteristic: Inherent characteristic of a product, process or system derived from a requirement.

Quality Control: The operational techniques and activities that are used to fulfil requirements for quality.

Quality costs: The expenditure incurred by the producer, by the user and by the community, associated with product or service quality.

Quality level: A measure of quality expressed in terms of a quantitative value such as proportion effective, percent non-conforming, parts per million, etc.

Quality loop: Conceptual model of interacting activities that influence the quality of a product or service in the various stages ranging from the identification of needs to the assessment of whether these needs have been satisfied.

Quality Manager: A person who is responsible for the manufacturer's Quality Management System (also sometimes referred to as the Chief Inspector).

Quality management: That aspect of the overall management function that determines and implements the quality policy.

  Note: The terms 'Quality Management' and 'Quality Control' are considered to be a manufacturer/supplier (or 1st party) responsibility. 'Quality Assurance' on the other hand has both internal and external aspects which in many instances can be shared between the manufacturer/supplier (1st party), purchaser/customer (2nd party) and any regulatory/certification body (3rd party) that may be involved.

Quality Management System: System to establish a quality policy and quality objectives and to achieve those objectives.

Quality Management System review: A formal evaluation by top management of the status and adequacy of the Quality Management System in relation to quality policy and new objectives resulting from changing circumstances.

Quality Manual: Document specifying the quality management system of an organisation and setting out the quality policies, systems and practices of an organisation.

Quality Plan: Document specifying the quality management system elements and the resources to be applied in a specific case.

Quality planning: Part of quality management focused on setting quality objectives and specifying necessary operational processes and related resources to fulfil the quality objectives.

Quality Policy: The overall quality intentions and direction of an organisation as regards quality, as formally expressed by top management.

Quality Procedure: A description of the method by which quality system activities are managed.

Quality records: Records should provide evidence of how well the Quality System has been implemented.

Quality system: The organisational structure, responsibilities, procedures, processes and resources for implementing quality management.

Quality system review: A formal evaluation by top management of the status and adequacy of the quality system in relation to quality policy and new objectives resulting from changing circumstances.

Record: Document stating results achieved or providing evidence of activities performed.

Requirement: Need or expectation that is stated, customarily implied or obligatory.

Review: Activity undertaken to ensure the suitability, adequacy, effectiveness and efficiency of the subject matter to achieve established objectives.

Service: Intangible product that is the result of at least one activity performed at the interface between the supplier and customer.
   Note: Service may involve, for example:

- an activity performed on a customer-supplied tangible (e.g. the repair of a car) or intangible (e.g. the preparation of a tax return) product;
- the delivery of a tangible product (e.g. in the transportation industry);
- the delivery of an intangible product (e.g. the delivery of knowledge) or the creation of ambience for the customer (e.g. in the hospitality industry).

Shall: This auxiliary verb indicates that a certain course of action is mandatory.

Should: This auxiliary verb indicates that a certain course of action is preferred but not necessarily required.

Supplier: The organisation that provides a product to the customer.

   Note 1.   In a contractual situation, the supplier may be called the contractor.
   Note 2.   The supplier may be, for example, the producer, distributor, importer, assembler or service organisation.
   Note 3.   The supplier may be either external or internal to the organisation.
   Note 4.   With regard to MDD the term Supplier is *not* used. The Directive instead refers to 'manufacturer'.

Top management: Person or group of people who direct and control an organisation at the highest level.

Work Instruction: A description of how a specific task is carried out.

USEFUL ADDRESSES

Members of the International Organization for Standardization (ISO) located within the EEC.

Austria (ON)

Österreichisches Normungsinstitut
Austrian Standards Institute
Heinestrasse 38
AT-1020 Wien
Tel: +43 1 213 00 610
Fax: +43 1 213 00 609
E-mail: **iro@on-norm.at**
Web: **http://www.on-norm.at/**

Belgium (IBN)

Institut belge de normalisation
Av. de la Brabançonne 29
BE-1000 Bruxelles
Tel: +32 2 738 01 11
Fax: +32 2 733 42 64
E-mail: **voorhof@ibn.be**
Web: **http://www.ibn.be**

Cyprus (CYS)

Cyprus Organization for the Promotion of Quality
Ministry of Commerce, Industry and Tourism
CY-Nicosia 1421
Tel: +357 22 40 93 06
Fax: +357 22 75 41 03
E-mail: **ikaris@cys.mcit.gov.cy**

Czech Republic (CSNI) Czech Standards Institute
Biskupsky dvur 5
CZ-110 02 Praha 1
Tel: +420 2 21 80 21 11
Fax: +420 2 21 80 23 11
E-mail: **extrel@csni.cz**
Web: **http://www.csni.cz**

Denmark (DS) Dansk Standard
(Danish Standards Association)
Kollegievej 6
DK-2920 Charlottenlund
Tel: +45 39 96 61 01
Fax: +45 39 96 61 02
E-mail: **dansk.standard@ds.dk**
Web: **http://www.ds.dk/**

Finland (SFS) Finnish Standards Association SFS
P.O. Box 116
FI-00241 Helsinki
Tel: +358 9 149 93 31
Fax: +358 9 146 49 25
E-mail: **sfs@sfs.fi**
Web: **http://www.sfs.fi/**

France (AFNOR) Association française de normalisation
11, avenue Francis de Pressensé
FR-93571 Saint-Denis La Plaine Cedex
Tel: +33 1 41 62 80 00
Fax: +33 1 49 17 90 00
E-mail: **uari@afnor.fr**
Web: **http://www.afnor.fr/**

Germany (DIN) DIN Deutsches Institut für Normung
Burggrafenstrasse 6
DE-10787 Berlin
Tel: +49 30 26 01-0
Fax: +49 30 26 01 12 31
E-mail: **directorate.international@din.de**
Web: **http://www.din.de**

Greece (ELOT)

Hellenic Organization for Standardization
313, Acharnon Street
GR-111 45 Athens
Tel: +30 210 21 20 100
Fax: +30 210 21 20 131
E-mail: **info@elot.gr**
Web: **http://www.elot.gr/**

Hungary (MSZT)

Magyar Szabványügyi Testület
Üllöi út 25
Pf. 24.
HU-1450 Budapest 9
Tel: +36 1 456 68 00
Fax: +36 1 456 68 23
E-mail: **isoline@mszt.hu**
Web: **http://www.mszt.hu/**

Ireland (NSAI)

National Standards Authority of Ireland
Glasnevin
IE-Dublin-9
Tel: +353 1 807 38 00
Fax: +353 1 807 38 38
E-mail: **nsai@nsai.ie**
Web: **http://www.nsai.ie**

Italy (UNI)

Ente Nazionale Italiano di Unificazione
Via Battistotti Sassi 11/b
IT-20133 Milano
Tel: +39 02 70 02 41
Fax: +39 02 70 10 61 49
E-mail: **uni@uni.com**
Web: **http://www.uni.com**

Luxembourg (SEE)

Service de l'Energie de l'Etat
Organisme Luxembourgeois de
Normalisation
34 avenue de la Porte-Neuve
B.P. 10
LU-2010 Luxembourg
Tel: +352 46 97 46 1
Fax: +352 46 97 46 39
E-mail: **see.normalisation@eg.etat.lu**
Web: **http://www.see.lu**

Malta (MSA)	Malta Standards Authority Second Floor, Evans Building Merchants Street MT-Valletta VLT 03 Tel: +356 21 24 24 20 Fax: +356 21 24 24 06 E-mail: **info@msa.org.mt** Web: **http://www.msa.org.mt**
Netherlands (NEN)	Nederlands Normalisatie-instituut Vlinderweg 6 NL-2623 AX Delft Postal Address P.O. Box 5059 NL-2600 GB Delft Tel: +31 15 2 69 03 90 Fax: +31 15 2 69 01 90 E-mail: **info@nen.nl** Web: **http://www.nen.nl**
Poland (PKN)	Polish Committee for Standardization ul. Swietokrzyska 14 PL-00-0050 Warszawa Tel: +48 22 556 75 91 Fax: +48 22 556 77 86 E-mail: **pl.isonb@pkn.pl** Web: **http://www.pkn.pl**
Portugal (IPQ)	Instituto Português da Qualidade Rua António Gião, 2 PT-2829-513 Caparica Tel: +351 21 294 81 00 Fax: +351 21 294 81 01 E-mail: **ipq@mail.ipq.pt** Web: **http://www.ipq.pt/**
Slovakia (SUTN)	Slovak Standards Institute P.O. Box 246 Karloveská 63 SK-840 00 Bratislava 4 Tel: +421 2 60 29 44 74 Fax: +421 2 65 41 18 88 E-mail: **ms_post@sutn.gov.sk** Web: **http://www.sutn.gov.sk**

Slovenia (SIST)

Slovenian Institute for Standardization
Smartinska 140
SI-1000 Ljubljana
Tel: +386 1 478 30 13
Fax: +386 1 478 30 94
E-mail: **sist@sist.si**
Web: **http://www.sist.si**

Spain (AENOR)

Asociación Española de Normalización y
Certificación
Génova, 6
ES-28004 Madrid
Tel: +34 91 432 60 00
Fax: +34 91 310 49 76
E-mail: **aenor@aenor.es**
Web: **http://www.aenor.es/**

Sweden (SIS)

SIS, Swedish Standards Institute
Sankt Paulsgatan 6
SE- Stockholm
Postal Address
SE-118 80 Stockholm
Tel: +46 8 55 55 20 00
Fax: +46 8 55 55 20 01
E-mail: **info@sis.se**
Web: **http://www.sis.se**

United Kingdom (BSI)

British Standards Institution
389 Chiswick High Road
GB-London W4 4AL
Tel: +44 208 996 90 00
Fax: +44 208 996 74 00
E-mail: **standards.international@
bsi-global.com**
Web: **http://www.bsi-global.com**

Other useful addresses

Canada (SCC)

Standards Council of Canada
270 Albert Street, Suite 200
CA-Ottawa, Ontario K1P 6N7
Tel: +1 613 238 32 22
Fax: +1 613 569 78 08
E-mail: **info@scc.ca**
Web: **http://www.scc.ca**

Croatia (DZNM)

State Office for Standardization and Metrology
Ulica grada Vukovara 78
HR-10000 Zagreb
Tel: +385 1 610 63 20
Fax: +385 1 610 93 20
E-mail: **ured.ravnatelja@dznm.hr**
Web: **http://www.dznm.hr**

Iceland (IST)

Icelandic Standards
Laugavegi 178
IS-105 Reykjavik
Tel: +354 520 71 50
Fax: +354 520 71 71
E-mail: **stadlar@stadlar.is**
Web: **http://www.stadlar.is**

ISO Central Secretariat

International Organization for Standardization
(ISO)
1, rue de Varembé, Case postale 56
CH-1211 Geneva 20, Switzerland
Tel: +41 22 749 01 11
Fax: +41 22 733 34 30
Web: **http://www.iso.org**

Norway (SN)

Standards Norway
Strandveien 18
NO-1366 Lysaker
Postal Address P.O. Box 242
NO-1326 Lysaker
Tel: +47 67 83 86 00
Fax: +47 67 83 86 01
E-mail: **info@standard.no**
Web: **http://www.standard.no**

**Russian Federation
(GOST R)**

State Committee of the Russian Federation
for Standardization and Metrology
Leninsky Prospekt 9
RU-Moscow, V-49, GSP-1, 119991
Tel: +7 095 236 40 44
Fax: +7 095 237 60 32
E-mail: **info@gost.ru**
Web: **http://www.gost.ru**

Serbia and
Montenegro (ISSM)

Institution for Standardization of Serbia and
Montenegro
Stevana Brakusa 2
Post. fah 2105
CS-11030 Belgrade
Tel: +381 11 54 70 96
Fax: +381 11 35 41 258
E-mail: **jus@jus.org.yu**
Web: **http://www.jus.org.yu**

Switzerland (SNV)

Swiss Association for Standardization
Bürglistrasse 29
CH-8400 Winterthur
Tel: +41 52 224 54 54
Fax: +41 52 224 54 74
E-mail: **info@snv.ch**
Web: **http://www.snv.ch/**

USA (ANSI)

American National Standards Institute
1819 L Street, NW
US-Washington, DC 20036
Tel: +1 212 642 49 00
Fax: +1 212 398 00 23
E-mail: **info@ansi.org**
Web: **http://www.ansi.org**

INDEX

Note: Page numbers in italics refer to figures and tables.